HURRICANES

HOW TO
PREPARE & RECOVER

Stories, photographs and illustrations
by the Staff of *The Miami Herald*

Book editing and design
by Max Roberts and Randy Stano
with special assistance from
Ana Lense-Larrauri, Dale Dupont, Kathy Foster

Andrews and McMeel
A Universal Press Syndicate Company
Kansas City

MW00718698

Hurricanes: How to Prepare and Recover, copyright ©
1993 by *The Miami Herald* Publishing Company, a division
of Knight-Ridder Inc. All rights reserved. Printed in the
United States of America. No part of this book may be
used or reproduced in any manner whatsoever without
written permission except in the case of reprints in the con-
text of reviews. For information, write Andrews and
McMeel, a Universal Press Syndicate Company, 4900
Main Street, Kansas City, Missouri 64112.

First Printing, May 1993

A percentage of Miami Herald profits from *Hurricanes:
How to Prepare & Recover* will go to hurricane relief
efforts.

Cover Design by Ana Lense-Larrauri

ACKNOWLEDGMENTS

This book was written and edited by the staff of *The Miami Herald.* Ideas and information came from readers and members of *The Herald.* Special thanks for time and energy go to artist Patterson Clark, Ana Lense-Larrauri and reporter Liz Leach.

These people specifically contributed to *Hurricanes: How to Prepare & Recover*:

ARTISTS AND DESIGNERS

Rick Brownlee, Patterson Clark, Dan Clifford, Bert Garcia, Tiffany Grantham, Hiram Henriquez, Alex Leary, Juan Lopez, Kim Marcille, Reggie Myers, Randy Stano and Woody Vondracek.

EDITORS AND REPORTERS

Fran Brennan, Gina Carroll, Tananarive Due, Dale Dupont, Don Finefrock, Kathy Foster, Felicia Gressette, Marty Klinkenberg, Liz Leach, Frank MacDonald, Doris Mansour, Alina Matas, Linda Roach Monroe, Jon O'Neill, Max Roberts, Bill Rose, David Satterfield, Terry Sheridan, Fred Tasker, Georgia Tasker, Bill Van Smith, Rich Wallace, Bill Wensel and Jo Werne.

LIBRARY RESEARCH

Gay Nemeti.

PHOTOGRAPHERS AND EDITORS

Marice Cohn Band, Candace Barbot, Peter Bosch, Dennis Copeland, Chuck Fadely, Patrick Farrell, Bill Frakes, C.W. Griffin, A. Brennan Innerarity, Beth Keiser, Jon Kral, Rick McCawley, Aladar Nesser, Walt Michot, Jon O'Neill, Joe Rimkus Jr., Jeffrey A. Salter, Mike Stocker, Charles Trainor Jr. and David Walters.

PRODUCTION

Kurt Moody, Paul Munro and John Payne.

Stripped: The Fort Lauderdale Beach at Los Olas Boulevard was left bare by Andrew; no people, no sun, no fun.

Cooling It: Marjorie Conklin rests in a bathtub that her brother dragged from the remains of her mobile home in Florida City.

Alone: At least one person faced the wind as Dania Beach was blasted by Andrew.

Hurricane Andrew stripped away South Florida's sticks and stones, sending roofs flying through neighbors' windows and scaring us into tiny closets clutching family, pets and a few treasures.

The painful months since August 1992 have revealed the strong character and courage of the people of South Florida in their struggle with the greatest natural disaster in U.S. history as measured in dollars.

It is also obvious — almost daily in The Herald's news stories — the necessity for us to build and rebuild better.

The staff of The Miami Herald and the many people who wrote us with helpful hints hope you will use this book to:

■ Examine and fix your home's weaknesses. Getting ready for a hurricane shouldn't be a last-minute job.

■ Gather supplies, protect family and secure windows as the storm approaches.

■ Safely recover without electricity, drinkable water and

A Crying Shame: Kids living in Eleuthera, the Bahamas, lost their home and their play area.

Gather Your Pets: Animals as well as people need attention and shelter, before, during and after a hurricane.

other supplies.

■ Repair your home and garden.

The Miami Herald has designated some of the profits from this book for hurricane relief efforts.

And, as you hammer a nail or two, rip a plywood sheet or trim trees, remember what Herald artist Ana Lense-Larrauri's mother, Mrs. Adela Lense, says when times are hard: "No hay mal que por bien no venga" (Good times follow the bad).

Help: This hornbill and many other valuable birds are still roaming South Florida skies.

Max Roberts
Home Editor

Randy Stano
Design Director

The Miami Herald

Table Of Contents

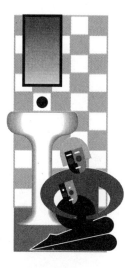

CHAPTER 1

What Is A Hurricane?

Reduce fear and know what to expect by studying what you should do — don't forget to track the storm.

Powerful Destruction

Hurricanes have been called the greatest storms on earth. It is not because they are the largest or the most powerful, but because they combine these traits.

The word ''hurricane'' is similar to the colonial Spanish and Caribbean words for evil spirits and big wind.

Hurricanes are tropical cyclones that move in a large spiral around the eye — the calm, low pressure center. Many begin as areas of low air pressure off the coast of Africa. These low pressure regions may grow into a tropical depression, with winds of up to 35 miles per hour; a tropical storm, with winds up to 72 mph, and finally, a hurricane with winds of 73 mph or more. The eye of the hurricane typically travels at 10 to 15 mph and the storm may extend 150 to 200 miles from the center.

The eye is the part of the hurricane to watch because it is deceptive. There, winds are light and skies are clear or partly cloudy. But people may find themselves caught in intense winds and torrential rains from the far side of the eye, where the wind blows from a direction opposite to that in the leading half of the storm.

Dangerous Path: In Homestead, exotic Australian pines looked like they had been mowed down. So many trees were damaged that one expert said it would take nurseries a decade to replace the lost foliage.

Hurricanes are rated from one to five according to disaster potential. All hurricanes are dangerous, some more than others. A Category One storm has minimum intensity; Category Five is the worst.

A hurricane's destructive power depends on how the storm surge — the rise in sea level — and wind combine. This combination can destroy buildings, erode beaches and produce massive floods.

Storm surge, the storm's worst killer, forms over the deepest part of the ocean and combines with the low pressure and strong winds around the hurricane's eye. Together, these three factors raise the ocean's surface up to two feet higher than the surrounding area, forming an arch of water that sometimes reaches out for 50 miles.

As the storm moves inland, over more shallow waters, the arch becomes a huge storm surge that can rise up to 20 feet above sea level and produce massive flooding.

Wind and associated tornadoes, and inland flooding are the next most dangerous aspects of the storm.

Wind force increases with the square of wind speed. For instance, when wind speed doubles, the wind force is four times as harsh on buildings and other structures.

Deadliest Hurricanes In History

1. Hurricane of Aug. 27 to Sept. 15, 1900 — 6,000 dead in Galveston, Texas.
2. Hurricane of Sept. 6 to 20, 1928 — 1,836 dead at Lake Okeechobee, Fla.
3. Hurricane of Sept. 2 to 15, 1916 — 790 dead on Gulf Coast and in shipwrecks.
4. Hurricane of Sept. 10 to 22, 1938 — 600 dead in New England.
5. "Labor Day Hurricane" of 1935 — 408 dead in Florida Keys.
6. Hurricane Audrey, June 1957 — 381 dead in Louisiana and Texas.
7. Hurricane of Sept. 14 to 21, 1909 — 350 dead in New Orleans.
8. Hurricane Camille, August 1969 — 323 dead from Mississippi coast to Virginia.
9. Hurricane Gilbert, September 1988 — 296 or more dead in Caribbean, Mexico, Texas.
10. Hurricane of Aug. 5 to 25, 1915 — 275 dead in Galveston.

HOW HURRICANES BEGIN

■ Tropical Depression
The tropical depression is the first step in creating a hurricane. Wind starts rotating in a pattern. As pressure begins to drop near the center, wind speed increases to 31 miles per hour. Narrow bands of rainfall form; some are heavy downpours.

■ Tropical Storm
A definite circular wind pattern develops. Warm, moist air is pumped into the weather system by wind speeds of up to 72 miles per hour. This causes heavy rainfall, and a pattern of squall lines develops.

■ Hurricane
An enormous pressure drop occurs in the center of the system. Monsoon-type rainfall occurs and the wind speed reaches a force of greater than 72 miles per hour. This causes gale-force winds that extend for hundreds of miles.

Over unusually warm seas near the equator in late summer, conditions are ripe for the formation of hurricanes.

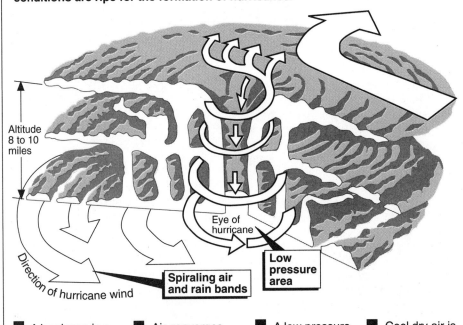

Altitude 8 to 10 miles

Eye of hurricane

Direction of hurricane wind

Spiraling air and rain bands

Low pressure area

■ A hurricane is a huge atmospheric heat pump that pulls in moist air from the ocean's surface.

■ Air converges in the center and spirals upward. The air is cooled and thunderstorms form.

■ A low pressure area forms on the ocean surface.

■ Cool dry air is cycled downward, where it is warmed by the sea and rises to continue the cycle.

Glossary

Annealed glass: common window glass.

Canopy: the top, leafy section of trees.

Category One Hurricane: winds of 73 to 95 miles per hour. Expected damage includes low-lying coastal roads inundated, small craft in exposed anchorages torn from moorings, some pier damage.

Category Two: winds of 96 to 110 mph. Damage estimates include coastal roads and low-lying escape routes inland cut off by rising water two to four hours before the arrival of the hurricane center. Marinas flooded. Some damage to windows, doors and roofing materials. Major damage to mobile homes.

Category Three: winds of 111 to 130 mph. Damages to include low-lying escape routes inland cut off by rising water three to four hours before the hurricane center arrives. Mobile homes destroyed. Some structural damage to small buildings. Serious coastal flooding.

Category Four: winds of 131 to 155 mph. Low-lying escape routes inland cut off by rising water three to five hours before arrival of the hurricane center. Major damage to lower floors of buildings near shore because of flooding and battering by waves and debris. Collapse of roofs on many small residences.

Category Five: winds of more than 155 mph. Low-lying escape routes inland cut off by rising water three to five hours before arrival of the center of the hurricane. Small buildings overturned or blown away. Extensive shattering of glass in windows and doors. Collapse of roofs on many residential and industrial buildings. Some buildings will collapse.

Chafing gear: rubber tubes, like sections of garden hose, covering mooring lines to protect against rubbing.

Conservation: a method of preserving what is left of an object. Conservation will not restore it to its original state.

Drop line: the electric cable leading from the street into a building.

Fascia: the wood strip nailed against the plywood joints of the roof.

Envelope: the outside structure of a building, including walls, roof, doors and windows.

Fender boards: lengths of boards with old tires lashed to one side and hung, tires next to the hull, over the side of the boat. They aid in protecting a moored boat from hull damage caused by other adjoining boats hitting it.

Flashing: a metal strip nailed over the first layer of roofing felt; it helps protect the edge and the paper from winds and rain.

Flood insurance: a type of insurance policy required in some areas by mortgage lenders. It covers the damage caused by rising water only, not water from leaky roofs or blown-out windows.

Gable roof: a roof style. The roof itself forms the two top sides of a triangle.

Gale warnings: issued in advance of a storm; winds of 38 to 55 mph are expected.

Hatrack: a method of trimming

Dennis Lavelle

"It would be a good idea to have a post-hurricane advice guide and include tips on the lessons we've learned since Andrew. A book could be written on Visqueen vs. those ubiquitous blue tarps. The blue marine tarps have eyelets and when anchored down would last several weeks. We stock up on flashlights and batteries, we should stock blue tarps too.

A week to 10 days after Andrew, Home Depot did an illustration showing how to do fundamental repairs to roofs. That was very helpful. You don't have to have a degree in roofing to know that water runs downhill. All people would have to do in order to 'dry in' their house would be to nail up some tar paper. Basically, for only $100 for some tin caps and roofing paper, homeowners would have been dry."

Marie O'Brian

"Wouldn't it be a good idea to have the teachers and faculty members correspond with schools in other cities [that have been affected by similar tragedies] and get the children involved.

Have them write pen pal letters to the children in Miami, expressing their own feelings and how they coped with the same problems, and give the kids their own views and encouragement.

Who better to communicate with children than other children their own ages."

trees by taking the top section off, leaving a rack of bare branches.

Hip roof: a roof with more than two sloping ends or sides.

Hurricane: a storm with a pronounced rotary circulation and a wind speed of at least 73 miles per hour. Based on disaster potential, hurricanes are rated from one to five. Category One has minimum intensity; Category Five is the worst.

Hurricane eye: the relatively calm

area near the center of a hurricane. Depending on the size and speed of the hurricane, it can take several minutes or several hours for the eye to pass. When it does, the calm ends suddenly and winds return, possibly with greater force, from the opposite direction.

Hurricane shutters: galvanized steel, aluminum, wood or plastic sheets used to protect sliding glass doors, entry doors and windows from airborne debris and wind pressure.

Hurricane straps: perforated metal strips embedded in the concrete tie beam and wrapped over the truss beams. They anchor the roof to the house and the trusses to the walls.

Hurricane warning: issued when hurricane is expected to strike within 24 hours.

Hurricane watch: a first notice; means a hurricane may threaten an area within 36 hours.

Laminated glass: a sandwich of two panes of glass with a center layer of plastic or fiber.

Marcite: the interior coating of

pools.

Mil: a unit of measure equal to 1/1000 (.001) meter, frequently used to measure the thickness of plastic.

Pitch: the angle, or slope, of the roof.

Plates: perforated metal panels that hold the joints of wood trusses together.

Pressed board: any of a variety of lumber manufactured by compressing sawdust or wood particles and a resin binding agent.

Replacement coverage: if an item is stolen or a portion of your house is damaged, the insurance company will pay for the replacement of that item or structure. There are two types. The most prevalent is replacement coverage with a predetermined cap. The insurer will replace items and the dwelling, but only up to a certain amount determined by the homeowner and agent. Guaranteed replacement coverage will replace all items, with no limit.

Restoration: total repair of an item. It may include adding elements not initially a part of the design.

Roofing felt: also known as tar paper or roofing paper; it is used to keep the water off the subroofing material. Several layers are needed. Common types are 15-, 30-, 60- and 90-weight or pound. Roofing plastic cement is used to adhere it to the subroofing.

Roofing staples: a substitute for nails. The staple is driven into the wood, generally with a staple gun. The teeth of the staple can be as long as nails, but are much thinner.

Screw anchors: a two-piece assembly used to fasten plywood to the outside of a building.

Shade cloth: material stretched

over plants to shield them from direct sun.

Shingle: a piece of asbestos, asphalt, fiberglass, slate, tile, wood or other material, cut or formed into a stock length, width and thickness for use as a roof or wall covering.

Shocking: a method of adding a chlorinator to pool water using 65 percent calcium hypochlorite granules.

Snubbing: using an elastic item in the middle of a mooring line to take up sudden shocks. Old motorcycle tires work well.

Soffit: the underside of the overhang of the trusses.

Storm warnings: notice that winds of 55 to 74 mph are expected.

Subroofing materials: the base portion of the roof; plywood and pressed particle board are most commonly used.

Tapinoma: a type of tiny, translucent ant commonly found in Florida.

Tempered glass: common window glass treated with heat to strengthen it.

Thermopane glass: a layer of air or gas sealed between panes of glass.

Tie beam: the anchor for the roof. Made of concrete, it should have steel bars running through the length of it.

Tile eave closure: a layer of cement under the first row of roof tiles. It prevents wind and water from entering.

Tin caps: Small, round, thin pieces of tin used with nails to hold down roofing

felt more effectively.

Transformer: an electric device with two or more coils of insulated wire, used to transfer AC power.

Transmission line: overhead or underground electric or telephone lines.

Tropical depression: a storm with winds to 39 miles per hour.

Tropical disturbance: a defined area of showers and thunderstorms that maintains its identity for 24 hours or more. It's the first sign of a potential hurricane.

Tropical storm: a storm with winds of 39 to 73 mph.

Trusses: the triangular support structure for roofs and ceilings. They also serve as horizontal braces for walls.

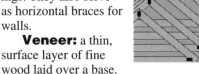

Veneer: a thin, surface layer of fine wood laid over a base.

Visqueen: a brand name for 6-mil-thick plastic. Often used to temporarily keep water off the sub-roofing materials.

Wound wood: the scab a tree forms over a fresh cut.

Kate Hale
Director, Dade County
Emergency Management
Office

"We need to do a better job of preparing our homes. Twenty-five percent of damage could have been avoided if people had just shuttered their windows. Andrew had a tight eye, a wide band of high winds, which is unusual. We would expect more rain from the next hurricane. We want people to think seriously of flooding, because that's what we'll see here next time."

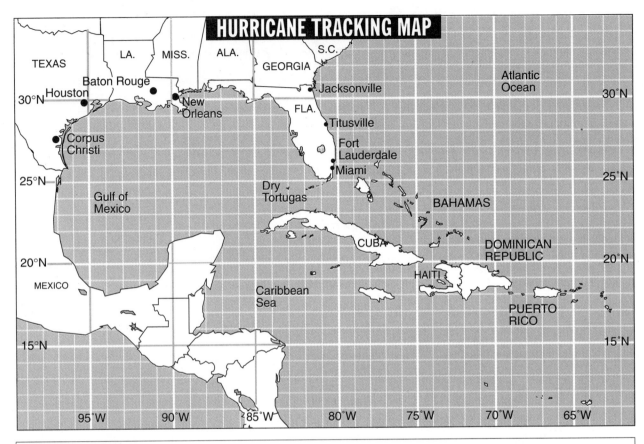

HURRICANE TRACKING MAP

STORM AT A GLANCE

DIRECTIONS: Listen for advisories from the U.S. Weather Bureau on tropical storms and hurricanes. Jot down the coordinate numbers (latitude and longitude positions). Locate the position of the storm center by the corresponding numbered latitude and longitude lines on the map. Circle the dot. As advisories continue, join the circles together to track the storm's path. List weather bulletin information below.

Number	1	2	3	4	5	6	7	8	9	10	11	12	13	14	15
Date															
Time															
Longitude															
Latitude															
Velocity (mph)															
Movement (mph)															
Direction															
Miles from Miami															

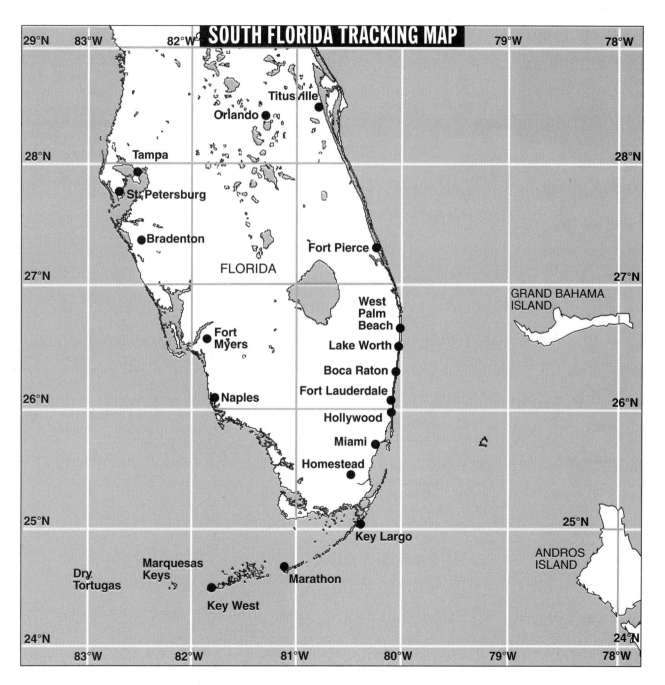

SOUTH FLORIDA TRACKING MAP

- 29°N
- 28°N
- 27°N
- 26°N
- 25°N
- 24°N

- 83°W
- 82°W
- 81°W
- 80°W
- 79°W
- 78°W

Titusville

Orlando

Tampa

St. Petersburg

Bradenton

FLORIDA

Fort Pierce

West Palm Beach

Lake Worth

Boca Raton

Fort Myers

Fort Lauderdale

Naples

Hollywood

Miami

Homestead

Key Largo

GRAND BAHAMA ISLAND

ANDROS ISLAND

Marquesas Keys

Dry Tortugas

Marathon

Key West

Henry Cisneros,
Secretary of Housing and
Urban Development

*"It will be two years
before we are through
with debris sweeps [in
South Dade] and a total
of five years before any
normalcy in Dade
County."*

What To Expect

If Andrew taught us anything, it was that the experts were right: Your best hurricane preparation is early hurricane preparation. Brace not only your home but also your family for a destructive storm well before one materializes. Otherwise, you could find yourself fighting hundreds of other people for the last gallon of bottled water or the last piece of plywood the night before a storm.

Make A Hurricane Checklist

■ Stock up on supplies to last at least a week, preferably two. Water is even more important than food, so stash at least seven gallons of water per person per week. Also include any medications family members need, food that doesn't require cooking, candles, batteries, a portable radio and, if possible, a gas or charcoal grill.

■ Secure your home with hurricane shutters for windows, doors and garage doors. Also plan to secure doors and garage doors from the inside so they don't blow in. Support the gable ends of your roof — most of those were lost during Hurricane Andrew.

■ Devise an evacuation plan. Decide where you will go if a hurricane threatens your home and plan to get there early. Assign each family member tasks — such as securing windows, packing clothes and bedding, filling the car with gas — to make the evacuation run more smoothly.

In The Event Of A Storm

■ Rely on newspapers, television and radio to provide details about weather conditions, evacuation sites and traffic problems. The media will relay any important announcements from local, state and federal governments. Many also will provide advice about securing your home and preparing for loss of power and water.

■ If a storm does enough damage to cause a state of emergency, expect the Federal Emergency Management Agency and nongovernmental relief organizations to provide water, food and shelter for those hardest hit. If the power is out, the portable radio and batteries in your hurricane kit will come in handy. Some television stations will broadcast on radio channels. And all media will alert residents to locations of shelters and relief centers.

■ Get to a relief site as quickly as possible after a destructive storm, especially if you do not have the supplies you need. From FEMA, the Red Cross, Salvation Army and others, you may be able to get water, ice, food, medical supplies, building supplies, shelter and even help repairing your roof.

■ Use print and broadcast media to help you cope. They will give you the information you need to survive and to find the things — and people — you may be missing because of the storm. Also look for tips on getting the most from the things you're left with, such as preserving cold food without power.

Who To Call

Following is a selection of agencies in South Florida that can provide assistance, or tell victims where to get help.

American Red Cross: (800) 498-0755, 8 a.m. to 5 p.m. Monday through Friday.

American Red Cross South Florida Region

Dade County: (305) 326-8888 8:30 a.m. to 5 p.m. Monday through Friday.

Broward County: (305) 763-9900 8:30 a.m. to 4:30 p.m. Monday through Friday.

Palm Beach County: (407) 833-7711 8:30 a.m. to 4:30 p.m. Monday through Friday.

The American Subcontractors Association of South Florida: (800) 329-7377, 8 a.m. to 5 p.m. weekdays.

Broward's Pupil Placement: (305) 765-6285, 7:30 a.m. to 5 p.m. Monday through Friday.

Broward-Palm Beach Apartment Association: (407) 998-8486, 9 a.m. to 5 p.m. Monday through Friday.

Centro Campesino: (305) 245-7738, 7:30 a.m. to 6 p.m. Monday through Saturday.

Children's Psychiatric Center: (305) 685-8244, 9:30 a.m. to 5 p.m. Monday through Friday.

Consumer Credit Counseling: — (305) 893-5225, 8:30 a.m. to 5 p.m. Monday through Friday.

Crisis Line Information and Referral for West Palm Beach: (407) 547-1000 or (407) 342-1000, anytime.

Dade County Building and Zoning: (305) 375-2500, 8 a.m. to 5 p.m. Monday through Friday.

Dade County School Board Help Line: (305) 995-Help, 8 a.m. to 4:30 p.m. Monday through Friday.

Epilepsy Foundation of South Florida: (305) 279-1100, 8:30 a.m. to 5:30 p.m. Monday through Friday.

Family Counseling Services: (305) 379-5720, 9 a.m. to 6 p.m. Monday through Friday.

Federal Emergency Management Agency: (800) 462-9029 5 a.m. to 7 p.m. daily; for the hearing impaired, (800) 462-7585.

FEMA Hotline: (Miami) — (800) 257-1407, 7 a.m. to 6 p.m. Monday through Friday.

First Call For Help in Broward: (305) 467-6333, anytime.

The Florida Department of Insurance: (800) 528-7094, 8 a.m. to 5 p.m. Monday through Friday.

The Florida Department of Professional Regulation: (800) 362-1519 or (800) 342-7940, 8 a.m. to 5 p.m. Monday through Friday.

Hialeah Children's Psychiatric Center: (305) 558-2480, 8:30 a.m. to 8 p.m. Monday through Thursday; 8:30 a.m. to 5 p.m. Friday.

Internal Revenue Service: (800) 829-3676, 8 a.m. to 5 p.m. Monday through Friday or (800) 829-1040, 8:15 a.m. to 5 p.m. Monday through Friday.

Mass Transit Information: (305) 638-6700, 6 a.m. to 10 p.m. Monday through Friday, 9 a.m. to 5 p.m. Saturday and Sunday.

The Miami Coalition for the Homeless: (305) 539-1641, 9 a.m. to 5 p.m. Monday through Friday.

North Dade Children's Psychiatric Center: (305) 685-0381, 8:30 a.m. to 8 p.m. Monday through

Kimberly Farr,
Age 11

"There's no way we would stay. I was so scared. Next time a hurricane comes, we'll be gone."

Sergio Bartoli

"What we need is more inspectors. The ones we have don't do their job. They let people put anything in and just turn their head. When property blows apart like it did down here, there are anchors missing. I think the only way you can have solid buildings is to have good honest inspectors — then you will have solid structures."

Thursday, 8:30 a.m. to 5 p.m. Friday and Saturday.

Salvation Army of Broward County: (305) 463-3725, 8 a.m. to 4 p.m. Monday through Friday, 8 a.m. to 1 p.m. Saturday.

Salvation Army of Dade County: (305) 643-4900, 8:30 a.m. to 4:30 p.m. Monday through Friday.

South Dade Children's Psychiatric Center: (305) 274-3172, 9 a.m. to 5 p.m. Monday and Tuesday, 9 a.m. to 7:45 p.m. Wednesday and Thursday, 9 a.m. to 12:45 p.m. Saturday.

Switchboard of Miami: a 24-hour crisis intervention and information referral source (305) 358-4357 anytime.

United Home Care Services: (305) 576-0308, 8 a.m. to 5 p.m. Monday through Friday.

United Way of America: (703) 836-7100, 8:30 a.m. to 6 p.m. Monday through Friday.

United Way of Dade County: (305) 579-2200, 8:30 a.m. to 5:30 p.m. Monday through Friday.

United Way of Broward County: (305) 462-4850, 8 a.m. to 5 p.m. Monday through Friday.

United Way of Monroe County: (305) 296-3464, 8 a.m. to 4 p.m. Monday through Friday.

United Way of West Palm and Delray Beaches: (407) 832-7300, 8 a.m. to 5 p.m. Monday through Friday.

Visiting Nurse Association of Dade County: (305) 477-7676, 8 a.m. to 5 p.m. Monday through Friday, answering service answers after 5 p.m. and on weekends.

Aground: Many boats moored at coastal marinas were badly damaged or blown ashore by Hurricane Andrew. Boaters are encouraged to seek refuge in inland waterways and reserve dock space at private facilities in protected areas.

Gloria Estefan

"A couple of times, we peered out through the lobby and the sound was so horrendous that we couldn't bear that, and we stayed in. At one point at about 3 in the morning, the whole building got sucked to the side. I was lying on the couch and my back got plastered to the couch. I thought, here we go. I've never seen anything like this in my life and I hope never to see it again. It was almost like they dropped the bomb, what I imagine people feel like in a war-torn city. It was very alien."

The Sounds And Fury

OK, so you're hunkered down in your house, hurricane shutters shut, doors locked and bolted, garage doors braced. What next?

It will vary, of course, according to the strength of the wind and the construction and location of your house. But there are several things — sounds, sights, sensations — to watch for as you cower in your battened down home.

First, whether it's day or night, expect your house to be dark and spooky. The shutters and the cloud cover will ensure that. So your view of the world within your house will be only as good as your candles and your flashlights.

The next thing one notices is the wind. It will be strong — but not just the strong thunderstorm gusts every South Floridian is familiar with. It will be even stronger and the noise — anything from a shriek to a howl to a continuous shhhhhh — will be unceasing. It will get on your nerves, but you may as well get used to it. It could last several hours. When you stop hearing it, the storm's over.

Lethal Missiles

You may hear a thumping sound, as if things are being blown into the sides of your house. You're right. They are. Tree limbs, pieces of metal, plywood sheathing from your neighbor's roof, asphalt shingles. All can become potentially lethal missiles when hurled by hurricane-force winds. Again, this intermittent clatter could last for hours.

Odds are you may hear the loud crack of tree limbs snapping — or even the ground-shaking whump of whole trees tumbling over. If any of these limbs or

trees hit your house, you'll know it immediately — from the crashing noise and shaking of the house at the very least and, at the worst, from the sudden sight of plaster, insulation and a wet tree plunging through your ceiling.

If the hurricane brings a lot of rain, you could experience the smell and messy sights and sounds of a sewer line backing up in your bathroom or sinks.

Depending on how close you are to the eye, your ears may start popping. Don't be frightened. It's caused by the change in atmospheric pressure — just like what happens when a 727 moves to a radically different altitude. A good swallow should clear your ears.

Don't Panic

Even though there are no windows broken and no obvious flaws in your defenses, you may feel a slight breeze inside your house and your candles may even blow out occasionally. Don't panic. That's just the wind's ability to find the tiniest holes in your house to blow through.

In a bad storm, even the best house may experience some shaking and creaking.

Garage doors may clang and clatter with the biggest gusts. Stay away from them unless you have them well braced. They have been known to collapse. And large limbs or other objects blown through the air make quite a racket as they strike the metal doors.

Listen carefully for the sound of running water. Let's hope you don't hear it. Unless you've left the water on, it means you have a leak. The storm has probably torn off some shingles or, worse, some of the plywood sheathing covering your roof. And the rain is pouring in. Pay particular attention to the corners of rooms on the outside of the house, and to light fixtures and fans. The leaks may show up there first.

If the storm penetrates your fortifications, you will know it. The wind will find its way in and look for ways to get out and so will the rain. Then you have a mess on your hands — wet and slippery floors, damaged carpets, damaged walls, damaged furniture, you name it.

Keep Talking

Dogs and cats may act funny. Primarily, they may hide or they may cling to you. There's not a lot you can do about that. Ever tried to reason with a dog or cat?

Over all this, hopefully, will come the sound of your link to the rest of the world — your battery-powered radio. Don't be without one. For one thing, it's comforting to hear another human voice. For another, it will allow you to keep up with where the storm is and how much more of it you can expect.

It is unnerving to sit in the dark and listen to and feel all of this chaos, to wait helplessly to see if your house can survive. If you're lucky enough and smart enough not to be alone, keep talking.

But keep one ear cocked for unusual sounds. They usually mean trouble.

Kristen Talavera,
Age 9

"My family filled a bathtub full of water. I think you should buy lots of drinking water. I also think you shouldn't wait until the night of the hurricane to buy everything you need because the stores will be very crowded. It is a good idea that you don't go into the refrigerator because the electricity will be out for quite a while. If you have any animals, you should bring them into the hall or any place with no windows. You should sleep in a place that has no windows. You should have batteries, a radio and a flashlight or lantern. If you board up your windows, put tape on first, so the glass won't shatter."

Feline Friend: Beloved pets were rescued from the rubble after the storm. If you must leave animals at home, put them in a secure room with dry food and water.

CHAPTER 2

Stormproof Your House

Don't wait! Shutters, valuables, insurance, plants need your attention now. Make lists, check them twice.

The Building Codes

The South Florida Building Code in Dade County was amended in key ways after Hurricane Andrew. Many of those changes apply to single-family homes.

Building code changes are anticipated in Broward County as well.

The Dade changes are effective for building permits dated May 1, 1993, or later, except for the code's new wind standard. That change is effective for building permits dated Jan. 1, 1994, or later.

Changes OKd In Dade

The code's 120-mile-per-hour wind standard was replaced with a national standard.

■ The 116-mph national standard is considered stronger because it takes wind gusts into account and factors how wind pressures build at certain points of a building, including roof edges and corners.

■ The design of single-family homes, and the products used to construct them, must be re-evaluated using the new standard.

■ Engineers say homes may be built with thicker roof trusses, more elaborate roof bracing systems, stronger window and door frames and more nails in the roof

Stocking Up: Bags of ice and charcoal are precious commodities before and after a storm. Get enough supplies to last at least a week, preferably two, including at least seven gallons of water per person per week.

decking as a result of the change.

■ Windows and doors on new homes must be strong enough to withstand hurricane winds and flying debris, or be protected by storm shutters.

■ Single-story homes built from concrete block must be anchored with columns of poured concrete.

■ Gable ends — the flat sides of pitched roofs — must be built from cement block, not wood, when the house is built from block.

In addition to these changes, Dade County adopted a temporary ban on the use of staples and pressed board as roofing materials because of questions about their performance during Andrew.

The county also set tougher standards for tile roofs and shingles, effective for all building permits issued on or after May 1, 1993.

Broward also imposed new requirements for roofing staples following Andrew, but did not ban their use. The county adopted new bracing requirements for wood-frame gable ends, but again stopped short of an outright ban.

The county's Board of Rules and Appeals is expected to consider additional changes in 1993.

For information on code requirements, call the Metro-Dade Office of Code Compliance at (305) 375-2901, from 7:30 a.m. to 5 p.m. weekdays; or the Broward Board of Rules and Appeals at (305) 765-4500, from 8 a.m. until noon and noon to 4:30 p.m. weekdays.

Andrew demolished roofs required to weather only 120 mph winds. In the zone of devastation, the neighborhoods that fared best were those whose roofs were better crafted.

TYPICAL ROOF CONSTRUCTION

Shingles are nailed or stapled through black **roofing felt** that is tacked down to plywood sheathing.

Tiles are cemented or nailed onto the roof.

Plywood decking acts as a support for roofing and a horizontal brace between trusses. It should be nailed firmly to supporting trusses.

Flashing is a metal strip nailed along the edge of the roof to protect the paper and sheathing from wind and water.

Trusses are triangular supports for roofing and ceilings. They also act as horizontal braces for walls.

Walls usually are concrete block. At the top of the wall, a reinforced concrete **tie beam** supports trusses.

Hurricane straps, embedded in the tie beam, are looped around and nailed to trusses.

STAGES OF DISINTEGRATION

On this home, erosion of the high roof began at the spot where a piece of flashing ripped away. Roofing felt and shingles soon followed.

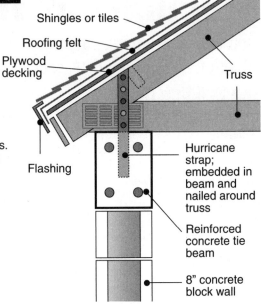

Shingles or tiles
Roofing felt
Plywood decking
Truss
Flashing
Hurricane strap; embedded in beam and nailed around truss
Reinforced concrete tie beam
8" concrete block wall

Over the master bedroom, plywood decking blew off, filling the house with wet, violent wind.

Composition shingles
Plywood decking
Roofing felt
Truss

Below: Without decking to brace them, trusses fell like dominoes. The interior of the home was devastated.

A structural engineer noted many examples of decking nails and staples missing their mark.

DECKING WITH STRONGER GRIP

Even though most of the barrel tiles were lost from this home, the plywood was held firmly in place by round-headed nails driven squarely into trusses.

GABLE VS. HIP

A roof's flat **gable end** met the winds head-on. Staples failed to hold the wafer board sheathing to the roof of this two-story house.

SOURCES: Zvonimir Belfranin, P.E.
Eugenio Santiago, P.E.
South Florida Building Code

A nearby neighbor's **hip roof** seemed to deflect the wind more effectively.

WHAT FAILED, WHAT PREVAILED

Examine your home for superior construction and hurricane-resistant features that enhance its survival possibilities. Here's what to look for when you examine an old house or a new.

THE ROOF

Surface roofing materials widely used include clay and concrete tiles, asphalt shingles and gravel. During Andrew, these materials failed when improperly attached or when shoddy maintenance allowed the wind to attack weaker portions.

Subroofing materials are the final defense if your tiles are torn off. Materials used currently include plywood and pressed particle board.

ROOF SURFACES

■ **Asphalt shingles** — Failure sometimes occurred due to installation damage. Tearing caused by staple guns left shingles with holes the storm tore further. Misplaced nails that did not allow the next shingle layer to lay flat also caused problems.

■ **Clay tiles** are more apt to shatter if hit by flying debris than concrete tiles. Loose tiles became projectiles and damaged others.

■ **Concrete flat tiles** experience some of the same problems as clay.

■ **Gravel roofs** endure if well maintained. Gravel roofs should be recoated with asphalt and gravel periodically. If not, the asphalt begins to flake off and sublayers may become exposed.

CLAY TILES

Asphalt felt underlayment

Plywood decking

Tile eave closure (cement)

Flashing

ASPHALT SHINGLES

Rafters

Asphalt cement

Roofing felt

Inverted starter strip

Fascia

ROOF STRUCTURE

Tiles/shingles nailed to the subsurface plywood decking. Additional techniques may be required by different types.

Roofing felt in several layers is the next layer of insulation against the elements.

Plywood or particle board decking nailed or stapled to trusses.

Fascia is a wood strip butting roof decking and nailed to truss ends.

Flashing is a metal strip nailed over the first layer of roofing felt. It protects the sheathing edge and paper from wind and rain.

Hurricane straps, 1/8-inch-thick strips of metal, anchor the roof to the house. They are embedded in the concrete tie-beam and nailed over the truss beams, connecting trusses to walls.

Concrete reinforced tie beam, with embedded steel bars running through its entire length, is the anchor for the roof.

Horizontal wind bracing, 2 by 4s connecting trusses at top and bottom, is often absent or inadequate in newer homes. Only some of the bracing system is indicated here. Extensive bracing helps a home to retain structural integrity under stress.

Decking should be firmly anchored to trusses with nails or staples. Nails are preferred over staples.

Trusses are supports for roofs/ceilings and are horizontal braces for walls.

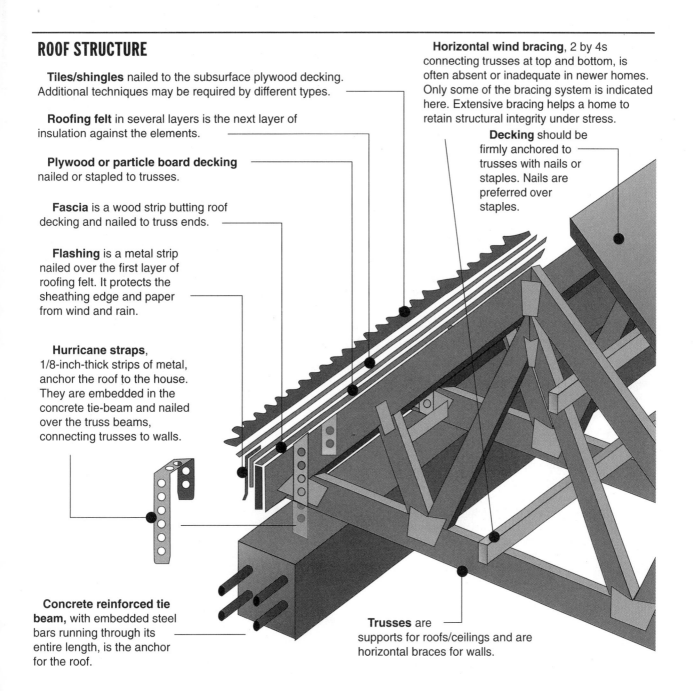

GABLE ROOF

HIP ROOF

WHAT DOES DESIGN CONTRIBUTE

HIP VS. GABLE

■ Hip roofs seem to deflect winds better than gable designs.
■ Gables seem to perform far better if they are entirely of masonry construction.

■ Steep roofs experienced structural failure at the peaks, lower roofs received damage at corners.

BLOCK VS. FRAME

■ Concrete block is more forgiving of poor craftsmanship than frame.
■ Blocks, even if badly put together, can still have more strength than wood framing.
■ The durability of frame construction is compromised if not designed

and put together well.
■ Poor wood framing may sometimes fail from the inside if hurricane winds get inside through shattered roof or windows.

PREFABRICATED ELEMENTS

■ Windows/doors that come framed as complete units must be carefully installed according to manufacturers' instructions.

■ Too often they are installed without reference to the manufacturers' shop drawings, resulting in failure.

WHY GABLE DESIGNS HAD TROUBLE

Gable ends made of concrete block are much more stable than wooden gable ends.

Horizontal bracing is very important to the structural integrity of the roof. Wooden gable ends must have more support than decking can provide.

Plywood decking is frequently used as the only horizontal stabilizer for gable ends and roof trusses. If the roof is penetrated, the structure may collapse.

SOURCES: John C. Pistorino, Miami engineer; Time Life Books; The Wood Truss Handbook.

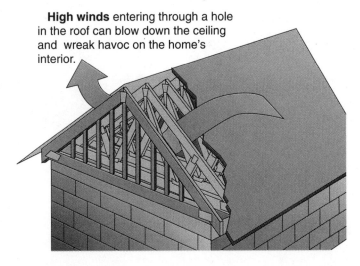

High winds entering through a hole in the roof can blow down the ceiling and wreak havoc on the home's interior.

Keep Track Of Your Possessions

A household should have a good system for storing important documents even without the threat of a storm. So organizing your papers before a storm might get you on track for a year-round system.

Irreplaceable Documents

Decide which papers in your house are irreplaceable. These might include pictures or letters with sentimental value or foreign documents replaceable only in their country of origin. For these, consider getting a bank safety deposit box — a small one rents for about $50 a year — and store them there.

A house vault — the kind that is anchored or embedded in the floor or wall of your house — is another alternative. However, a loose safety box that can be blown away does not offer much security.

Also store in the vault:

■ Original ownership documents, such as the title on your house or car.

■ Original bond and stock issues.

■ Birth certificates, particularly if from another country.

Replaceable Documents

Many business documents, such as bank or insurance records, can be duplicated by the companies that issued them, should they be totally destroyed in a hurricane. The same goes for medical records and public records such as marriage certificates.

However, it will save you time and aggravation to safeguard some basic documents. Protecting replaceable documents — or at least the essential information in them — will avoid your having to rely on the issuers to locate and duplicate them for you.

What To Do

Gather originals and make copies of:

1. A document that shows the name of your insurance company and your insurance policy number. It could be the insurance binder or your last bill.

2. A piece of paper with the name, address and phone number of your insurance agent.

3. Receipts or canceled checks for home furnishings that might be damaged. The receipts, if you have them, will help you document your losses on your insurance claims and tax deduction claims.

4. Photographs of each of the rooms of your house, showing the furnishings in each. Again, this will come in handy when making insurance claims and tax deduction claims.

5. A document that shows the name, address and phone number of your mortgage holder and your account number.

6. Any other documents that show proof of value, such as a recent assessment of your home.

Portable Kit

■ Get two 8-by-11 manila envelopes. Stuff the originals in one envelope. Stuff photocopies in the other envelope.

■ Keep the envelope with originals in the same place where you plan to stay throughout the storm.

■ Give the envelope with the copies to a friend or relative who lives outside your area, or keep it at your place of work.

■ After the storm, the envelopes with phone numbers and account numbers will be your portable phone-call making kit.

Joseph B. Scott

"1. Make out a home inventory list of all your belongings before hurricane season. Take pictures, and/or videotape of all your belongings, and your house inside and out. Store a copy of your home's blueprints, or make out a floor plan. Include any improvements.

2. Have two ice coolers on hand. If the electricity is out for several days, your refrigerator will be useless. If you have two coolers, you can store your food in one, and go for more ice with the other.

3. New plastic trash cans make a great place to store extra water. They are clean, water tight, and the lid keeps the water somewhat clean.

4. A great food to store for a storm is the microwave meal in a cup. Don't let the word microwave keep you away. These are precooked, ready -to -eat meals in an airtight container with a pull- top lid."

You May Also Safeguard:

■ **Canceled checks:** Although a bank can replicate these from microfiche, to save hassle and expense, consider protecting these from rain and wind. Store or wrap in plastic, and put in a part of the house likely to survive wind and rain.

How much of a history of canceled checks you want to keep is up to you. Some accountants recommend keeping as far back as seven years.

■ **Medical records:** Such as the children's vaccinations history.

■ **Marriage license and certificate**.

One More Safeguard

■ Photocopy all the cards you keep in your wallet: driver's license, credit cards, medical insurance cards, ATM cards. On the photocopies of your bank cards, write the phone number for reporting a lost card.

Should you lose your wallet, the photocopies will make reporting and replacing much easier.

Your Possessions

Don't wait for the storm's approach to catalog your possessions. Now is the time to make a list, and check it twice, of what you own. In each room, we've given you some ideas; please add other items at the bottom of each page.

MISCELLANEOUS

Item	Number of items	Date acquired	Cost or other basis	Fair market value before casualty	Fair market value after casualty	Decrease in fair market value

LIVING ROOM

Item	Number of items	Date acquired	Cost or other basis	Fair market value before casualty	Fair market value after casualty	Decrease in fair market value
Accessories						
Blinds						
Bookcases						
Books						
Chairs						
Chests						
Clocks						
Coffee table						
Curtains						
Desk						
Draperies						
Lamps						
Mirrors						
Pictures						
Pillows						
Radio						
Rugs and pads						
Shades						
Shutters						
Sofa						
Stereo						
Television						
Wall fixtures						

DINING ROOM

Item	Number of items	Date acquired	Cost or other basis	Fair market value before casualty	Fair market value after casualty	Decrease in fair market value
Buffet						
Chairs						
China cabinet						
Chinaware						
Crystal						
Curtains						
Draperies						
Glassware						
Mirrors						
Pictures						
Rugs and pads						
Silver flatware						
Silver tea set						
Silver items						
Table						
Wall fixtures						

Item	Number of items	Date acquired	Cost or other basis	Fair market value before casualty	Fair market value after casualty	Decrease in fair market value
Blender						
Broiler						
Canned goods						
Can opener						
Clock						
Coffee maker						
Curtains						
Cutlery						
Dishes						
Dishwasher						
Food processor						
Freezer						
Frozen food						
Glassware						
Microwave oven						
Mixer						
Pots and pans						
Radio						
Refrigerator						
Stove						
Table and chairs						
Telephone						
Toaster						
Utensils						
Wall accessories						

KITCHEN

BEDROOMS

Item	Number of items	Date acquired	Cost or other basis	Fair market value before casualty	Fair market value after casualty	Decrease in fair market value
Bed covers						
Beds						
Bedside tables						
Bureaus						
Chairs						
Chests						
Clocks						
Clothes hamper						
Desks						
Dresser						
Jewelry box						
Lamps						
Linens						
Mirrors						
Pictures						
Radio						
Rugs and pads						
Telephone						
Television						

RECREATION ROOM

Item	Number of items	Date acquired	Cost or other basis	Fair market value before casualty	Fair market value after casualty	Decrease in fair market value
Bookcase						
Books						
Card table						
Chairs						
Clocks						
Computers						
Desks						
Games						
Lamps						
Pictures						
Ping pong table						
Pool table						
Radio						
Records						
Rugs and pads						
Sofa						
Stereo						
Tables						
Telephone						
Television						
Video recorder						

BATHROOMS

Item	Number of items	Date acquired	Cost or other basis	Fair market value before casualty	Fair market value after casualty	Decrease in fair market value
Bath mats						
Clothes hamper						
Curtains						
Hair dryer						
Linens						
Mirrors						
Pictures						
Razor						
Scales						
Towel rack						
Wall fixtures						

GARAGE

Item	Number of items	Date acquired	Cost or other basis	Fair market value before casualty	Fair market value after casualty	Decrease in fair market value
Bicycles						
Garden hose						
Garden tools						
Hedger						
Ladder						
Lawn mower						
Sprayer						
Spreader						
Tools						
Wheelbarrow						

Renters' Problems

For renters, preparing for the next storm means getting insurance.

No matter where you live, renting an apartment or condo without insurance just doesn't make sense. For just a few hundred dollars a year, renters can replace their lost, stolen or damaged belongings after a crisis. Without it, renters will be left out in the cold.

Even if your loss was caused by damage to the physical structure of an apartment building, such as during the hurricane, a renter's loss will not be covered by the apartment complex's insurance. These policies cover the buildings, not tenant's personal property. Likewise, a condo association's insurance does not cover personal belongings.

Insurance Survey

A post-hurricane Andrew survey commissioned by The Miami Herald found that only 6 percent of renters in South Dade carried insurance for the contents of their dwellings. Census figures showed that 46 percent of the households in Dade County at that time were occupied by renters.

For only a few dollars a day, those hurricane victims would not have had to start from scratch.

It's best to buy a replacement value policy. Just like a car that depreciates the minute you drive out of the showroom, your belongings lose value as they are used.

With a replacement value policy, the insurance company will give you the money it would cost to purchase the item new again, rather than what it may actually be worth.

Basics To Cost More

Be prepared to pay more for basic coverage if you live on the water. Many companies will not insure renters living on the ocean or Intracoastal.

Basic policies limit the amount of coverage on items such as jewelry and computers, but you can get more coverage if you are willing to pay more.

For example, State Farm has limited losses on jewelry to $1,000. If your jewelry is worth more than that, you can buy a rider to cover the extra value. For less than $50 more, you can buy coverage of $1,500 per item, or $2,500 per loss.

Electronic items such as televisions and VCRs are covered under the basic policy, but coverage for computers is limited to $5,000. You can double that coverage for about $15.

Be sure to tell the agent about home business supplies, watercraft, silverware, rugs, tapestries and any special items you may have, such as a coin or other valuable collection. Bills of sale, proofs of purchase with descriptions and appraisals of valuable items are important tools for filing a claim.

Keep Receipts

It's a good idea to inventory your belongings and keep receipts for everything. Photographs, videotapes or written descriptions are important to document your loss and help police identify stolen merchandise.

The items listed in the inventory will be covered by the policy if they are lost, damaged or stolen from your home, car, on an airplane or in another country.

Bob Sheets,
Director of National
Hurricane Center

He warns that despite hurricane Andrew "too many people don't take the threat of another storm seriously enough. There's a false sense that the reason for the damage was because somebody didn't put a nail in right. The perception is for people to say 'my house is built fine so I don't have a problem.' Well, 90 percent of those damaged buildings met code. You're just going to get that kind of damage when you have that kind of wind."

Insurance List

Insurance may be one of the few consolations you have after the storm. Here are some tips to make dealing with companies less confusing.

■ Contact your agent as quickly as possible.

■ Find and read your homeowners or renters insurance policy.

■ Tell the insurer if you're in an emergency situation.

■ Policies usually pay for three things: additional living expenses if you're displaced, temporary repairs to protect your home and the actual value and replacement value of damaged property. You may get two checks — one for the contents and one for the structure.

■ Many policies don't pay for debris removal. However, if a tree falls on your home, your insurance policy might pay for its removal.

■ Flood damage caused by rising water is covered under flood insurance, which is required in some areas if you have a mortgage. The federal government underwrites flood insurance, but most insurance adjusters can handle the claims. Ask your agent about flood coverage.

Insurance

Andrew awakened South Florida to the need for good insurance, a good insurance carrier, and a wise insurance agent.

Unfortunately, the hurricane also has made insurance more difficult and more confusing than ever before.

Here are some questions likely to face homeowners in coming months.

■ Is my current insurance adequate?

Review your policy. Determine exactly what you're entitled to in the event of a fire or catastrophe.

Most experts say people should get insurance that allows them to rebuild their home at today's prices. They should buy coverage that pays replacement value of their personal goods. And they should get coverage for living expenses if they can't live in their home.

If you have other special items such as jewelry or backyard sheds, decide whether you want them insured. If so, buy special coverage.

■ What's the best type of policy?

A guaranteed replacement policy is the best coverage, because it is supposed to guarantee that the insurance company will pay to rebuild your house and replace your contents, no matter the cost. These policies may be difficult to find after Andrew.

The most widely available form of coverage is the replacement-cost policy. It will replace your home and contents, but only up to a certain predetermined cap.

Many companies also will insure your home and contents for their actual cash value. Under these policies, the company depreciates the value of the damaged item and pays you that amount. Most experts warn consumers against buying such policies.

■ What if my home has increased in value?

Make sure the coverage has increased accordingly. And remember, the value of your home may be less than what it costs to rebuild the same home. Insurers usually figure you can rebuild your home for about 80 percent of the value of your home and land. But that's not always the case.

Check around for construction prices, and estimate how much you would need to rebuild. Remember this lesson from Andrew: Construction prices always go up after a hurricane.

■ What about my personal belongings?

Most homeowner policies limit coverage of personal contents to 50 percent of the amount of the insurance on the home. If the home is insured at $100,000, personal contents are insured at $50,000. Don't settle for that coverage if you know your contents are worth more.

■ What's a good deductible?

That depends on your personal circumstances. Many people carry low deductibles so they don't have to pay much money if they're victims of thieves or storms. Others choose high deductibles because it reduces the cost of insurance. Consult with your agent about which deductible best fits your needs.

■ What if I can't find homeowner insurance?

The state has created a special ''joint

underwriting association'' or JUA, to sell last-ditch coverage. Thousands of agents are selling the policies, and eight insurance companies will process the applications and handle claims.

■ What if I have insurance?

Most companies say they will continue to insure existing customers. But a handful, including industry giant Prudential Property & Casualty, are canceling many policies when they come up for renewal. Those people should look for new coverage elsewhere, but may be forced to buy a JUA policy.

■ What if I live east of Interstate 95 or east of U.S. 1 in South Dade?

You may be forced to buy a special policy that insures your home against hurricanes. Because of the shortage of insurance in South Florida, the state expanded the Florida Windstorm Underwriting Association into the eastern part of Dade and Broward. The association, which is similar to the JUA, sells coverage against hurricanes and hailstorms. You buy a policy from the wind pool, as it's called, and a separate policy from either the JUA or a private company. Prudential, for instance, is forcing all of its customers in eastern Dade and Broward to buy wind pool coverage. Prudential then will insure those homes against all other risks.

■ Is the JUA and windstorm coverage any good?

It's better than nothing, but not nearly as good as a normal policy. They are more limited than the products available before the storm.

For instance, the policies will only insure homes up to $500,000. The minimum deductible is $500. The JUA policy offers to replace a home, but only up to a specific value determined by the homeowner. There is no provision to guarantee total replacement of a home.

The JUA policy does not pay replacement costs on personal contents. It only pays the actual depreciated value of those belongings.

The windstorm policy offers even less coverage. Homeowners can choose from several options, but they don't even get replacement cost of their home if a hurricane strikes. Instead, the best they can get is 90 percent of their loss.

The wind policy also does not pay for additional living expenses if a home is uninhabitable. The JUA policy will provide those expenses. Prudential said its nonhurricane policy also will pay living expenses, even if the home is damaged in a hurricane.

■ Are the JUA and wind policies cheaper than regular insurance?

No, together they are at least 25 percent more expensive than a normal policy. The JUA keeps its prices high to encourage homeowners to get coverage from private insurers. And the JUA's higher prices encourage private companies to get back into the insurance business in Florida.

■ When will things return to normal?

If another hurricane hits Florida, things won't return to normal for a long time. But most experts think the insurance shortage will last about two years. Then, insurance companies will be eager to go after the estimated $1 billion in homeowner premiums Florida residents pay each year.

Insurance List, Cont'd.

■ Only make repairs necessary to prevent further damage to your home or business. Don't make permanent repairs without consulting your agent.

■ An insurance adjuster will make an appointment to visit your home. It may take days or weeks. Be patient.

■ Before the adjuster arrives, prepare a list of damaged and destroyed personal property. The list should include a description of the item, date of purchase or age, cost at time of purchase and estimated replacement cost. If you have canceled checks or receipts for those items, collect them to show the adjuster.

■ If possible, get a detailed estimate for repairs.

■ Take photographs or videos of the damaged areas.

■ Keep all receipts for all work done on your home.

■ The Florida Department of Insurance has a hot line to handle complaints or questions. The number is (800) 528-7094. It is staffed from 8 a.m. to 5 p.m.

Peter Disch-Lauxman

"While our Whispering Pines neighborhood was virtually destroyed, we survived Andrew with less than $1,000 damage to the house itself. We have steel bars mounted to the inside walls just between two and three inches behind the windows. All windows were protected from the outside with aluminum storm panels and from the inside with cut-to-size pieces of plywood tied with wire to the steel bars. After two aluminum panels broke away and the windows behind shattered, the plywood tied to the bars kept wind force and most of the rain out of the house."

Two Methods For Making Plywood Window Covers

One-Sheet Windows

If the window is no more than 3 feet by 4 feet, one sheet of plywood — at least one half inch thick — will cover it.

You will not need to make a framework around the window, as you would for multiple sheets.

That single sheet must include an overlap around the window of at least 4 inches on all four sides. The reason: The very edge of the window opening won't provide sturdy anchoring.

■ **Predrill:** Lay the plywood sheet flat and drill (using the wood bit) holes for the anchor 18 inches on center — keeping in mind a 4-inch overlap from the window opening.

Starting from one corner of the sheet, measure 18 inches — and drill a hole every 18 inches.

Hold the sheet up to the window; stick a pencil through each drilled hole, marking the concrete/ stucco.

■ **Anchors:** Set the sheet aside, and use the masonry bit to drill holes for the anchors where you made the pencil marks.

One-inch-deep is good, but note that the lags, shields, or wedge anchors you buy may require deeper.

Tap the anchors into each hole with a hammer. As you tap wedge anchors, for instance, they spread inside the hole and tighten.

■ **Cover:** Place the plywood sheet over the window, matching the predrilled holes with those just drilled for the anchors. Push the bolts through the holes into the anchors. Use the drive socket to tighten the bolts.

Multisheet Windows

If the size of a window requires more than one sheet of plywood to cover it, you'll first need to build a framework to which you will attach the cover.

This is because the seams between sheets must be braced, and that brace should rest within the anchored frame.

■ **Framework:** Measure your window on all four sides, allowing a 4-inch overlap beyond the window opening.

Use the saw to cut a 2-by-2 or a 2-by-4 to fit each side of the opening. The boards do not have to be mitered to fit like a picture frame, but corners should be close to each other. Two-by-fours allow more space for drilling wood screws. If you use 2-by-4s, lay them flat around the window on their widest side, not standing on their narrow sides.

■ **Predrill:** After measuring and cutting frame pieces, lay them flat. Using the wood bit, drill the bolt holes 18 inches on center. (Again, this means that, starting from one corner of the sheet, you measure 18 inches — and drill a hole every 18 inches.)

Hold the frame pieces up around the window. Stick a pencil through each drilled hole, marking the concrete/ stucco. These marks will tell you where to drill the anchor holes.

■ **Anchors:** Set the frame pieces aside, and use the masonry bit to drill holes for the anchors where you made the pencil marks.

One inch is a good depth, but the lags/ shield/ wedge anchors may require a deeper hole.

Tap the anchors into each hole with a hammer.

Now, bolt each frame piece into place — sliding the bolts into the holes you predrilled in the frame and on through into the anchor holes. Use the drive socket to tighten the bolts.

■ **Brace:** Each seam between pieces of plywood cover will require a brace behind it.

Even if you've opted for 2-by-2s for the framework, use a 2-by-4 for the brace. The greater width will better accommodate the screws required to attach the two sheets on either side of the brace.

The brace is placed vertically over the window. The brace should fit snugly between the top and bottom framework. If you're using a 2-by-4, be sure to lay it flat.

Failure to provide braces will defeat the purpose of the covers because the loose ends of the plywood either will bang against the windows and break them, or

allow the wind to rip the entire sheet off the house.

■ **Cover:** Lay the plywood sheet flat and, using the wood bit, drill the screw holes 6 inches on center. (Drill a hole every 6 inches around the sheet.)

Then hold the sheet up to the framework, and mark those screw holes with a pencil onto the framework.

You can drill a pilot hole in the framework to start the screw.

Screw the No. 10 wood screws through the plywood cover into the framework and brace.

A 6-foot-wide, 7-foot-tall sliding glass door, using two sheets of plywood, could require 82 screws — 13 across the top and bottom, 14 on each side and the two sides that must be attached to the brace.

General Tips

■ With several windows of the same size, the plywood sheets and framework can be interchangeable. Otherwise, number the framework and cover sheets to correspond with the openings.

■ Drill the anchor holes and set the anchors now. Don't try to do all this as a storm is approaching. The holes can be protected by filling them with a soft caulk, such as silicone; use an ice pick to clean them when you need to hang plywood sheets.

■ For sliding glass doors, extend the bottom framework several inches beyond the edge of the door to provide extra support. This is because it is difficult, if not impossible, to anchor the bottom frame to any part of the door or door track.

In this case, nail the brace to the bottom frame. Then anchor each side of the frame that extends beyond the opening to the concrete. Now raise the brace. It should fit snugly up under the top frame.

Cover Up: Shield windows from flying debris with wood or other shutters. One sheet of plywood, for example, will cover windows no more than 3 feet by 4 feet. If a window requires more than one sheet of plywood, first build a framework to which you will attach the cover.

CHOOSING HURRICANE SHUTTERS

This guide offers a look at the costs, as well as the benefits and drawbacks, of eight varieties of hurricane shutters.

PLYWOOD SHUTTERS

Often homemade, these are sheets of plywood at least half-inch thick that must be cut to fit snugly over window and door openings. To work, they must be properly fastened over windows. They should be precut and predrilled so they can be fastened to anchors installed in the house when a storm approaches.

Performance: Plywood shutters can provide excellent protection but only if securely fastened. Many homeowners who hastily nailed plywood over windows before Andrew found their shutters in neighbors' yards after the storm. Plywood is difficult to store and handle.

Cost: The cheapest alternative for a do-it-yourselfer: you can cut and install coverings for a 6-foot wide sliding glass door for about $50, including the screws and anchors. Covering a 37-inch by 50-inch window would cost about $25.

HORIZONTAL ROLLING SHUTTERS

Top and bottom tracks are attached to the wall. The tracks extend horizontally beyond the window opening. The shutter slides along the tracks. Before a storm, slide shutters over the window and fasten them to the tracks with clips.

Performance: These typically don't require a storm bar, because the shutters slide on a track that is permanently attached to the house. They require minimal preparation before the storm and no storage.

Cost: A 6-foot sliding glass door costs about $1,000. For a 37-inch by 50-inch window, figure on about $400.

COLONIAL-STYLE SHUTTERS

Decorative louvered shutters, which are attached to the side of the window. Can be made to look like wood. When the storm comes, shut them and screw storm bars on the top and bottom to fasten the shutters to the wall.

Performance: Require minor preparation, although you still have to attach the storm bars before the storm. If solidly made, can protect adequately.

Cost: For a 6-foot wide sliding glass door, it would cost about $800. For a 37-inch-wide by 50-inch-long window, about $270.

ALUMINUM AWNINGS

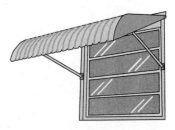

They are permanently on top of the window. Before the storm, the awning folds down over the window and is anchored to the wall with screws.

Performance: They work well, if made of thick aluminum and fastened properly. They are convenient because they are permanently attached and require minor preparation at storm time.

Cost: About the middle of the range of options. An awning for a 6-foot sliding glass door would cost about $400. For a 37-inch by 50-inch window, it would cost between $160 and $180.

BAHAMA-STYLE SHUTTERS

A decorative, louvered shutter, permanently attached above the window. Can be made to look like wood. The entire shutter hangs low over the window. For storm protection, the shutter is lowered and fastened to a storm bar at the bottom. Can be made to look like wood.

Performance: These are easy to fasten before the storm. They require no storage. However, because of the design, they are not feasible for sliding glass, garage or entry doors. They should provide protection if solidly manufactured and fastened properly.

Cost: For a 37-inch by 50-inch window, cost would be about $250.

STORM PANELS

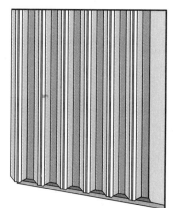

A track is installed permanently above the window or door. When the storm approaches, use screws to fasten a storm bar to the bottom, then slide one-foot aluminum or steel panels along the top track and fasten them to the bottom storm bar.

Performance: Overall, these get high ratings. The panels are easy to handle and store. Some experts favor steel, because it's stronger. Others say aluminum can perform adequately and is lighter and easier to handle.

Cost: One of the least expensive options. Panels for a 6-foot sliding glass door would cost between $225 and $350, depending on the thickness of the aluminum. For a 37-inch by 50-inch window, the panels would cost between $80 and $120.

ROLL-DOWN SHUTTER

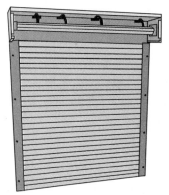

The shutter is rolled inside a horizontal casing attached permanently above a window or door. Before the storm, roll down the shutter and fasten it to a storm bar. Some styles require additional storm bars. Mechanisms can be hand-cranked or electronic.

Performance: At least in theory, they should be effective if manufactured with high-quality materials. However, one shutter business owner said many roll-downs failed in the hurricane, perhaps because of improper attachment of the storm bars. They are convenient — all you do is roll down. You still have to attach storm bars for large windows or doors.

Cost: The most expensive style. For a 6-foot sliding glass door, it would cost between $1,000 and $1,300, depending on the thickness. For a 37-inch by 50-inch window, it would cost between $450 and $750. An electronic motor would add between $200 and $400.

ACCORDION DOORS

This shutter folds against the side edge or at the center of the window or door. When the storm comes, expand the shutter out and fasten it.

Performance: In one condo, these performed as well as roll-down shutters. In cases where they failed, the thickness of the aluminum and improper fastening could have made the difference. One convenience: The entire system is attached, so no storage is required.

Cost: For a 6-foot sliding glass door, cost ranges between $600 and $800, depending on the thickness of the aluminum. For a 37-inch by 50-inch window, it would cost between $200 and $260.

Bryan Norcross

The first thing that Bryan Norcross did when he first bought his house in Coconut Grove was to install storm shutters.

"I didn't want to look stupid. The hurricane was the most stressful moment in [everyone's] lives. To be in fear of what's going to happen in the next 10 minutes, in the dark, afraid for your life. This was a once-in-a-lifetime event, I hope."

What You Will Need

Here is a shopping list for making plywood window covers.

Prices are guidelines.

■ Tape measure long enough to measure windows and doors, under $10.

■ Screwdrivers, flat head or Phillips depending on the type of bolts you buy, under $5.

■ Electric drill, from about $35 to more than $100.

■ Saw, about $6 to $19.

■ Masonry and wood drill bits, under $5. Industrial/ commercial drills typically have chucks (the opening for the bit); a general, homeowner-grade drill may have a chuck. Make sure the bit you buy has a shank (or bottom) that fits your drill's chuck.

The size bit you need will depend on the type of anchor used. A masonry bit is good because wedge anchors typically are one-half inch in diameter. But will that bit work with your drill?

■ Wedge anchors and bolts, under $2 for this use. You need an anchor and a bolt that will attach the framework to the anchor. A wedge is one type of anchor to use. There also are lags (or lag shields) and lag or carriage bolts, and others. Depending on what type of bolt selected, you may also need washers. Steel anchors are best.

■ Hammer, from $10 to $30.

■ Socket wrench set, about $20. (You can buy individual drive sockets.) While the size of the drive socket will depend on the size of bolt used with the anchor, you'll most likely need a drive socket.

■ No. 10 wood screws, 1-inch, 69 cents for a bag of six screws. (A 6-foot-wide, 7-foot-tall sliding glass door, using two sheets of plywood, could require 82 screws: 13 across the top and bottom, 14 on each side and the two sides that must be attached to the brace.)

■ Plywood sheets, at least one-half-inch thick, $12.05 for a 4-foot by 8-foot sheet; $18.45 for the same size thick.

■ 2-by-2s or 2-by-4s, about $2 for a 2-by-2-by-8; about $3 for a 2-by-4-by-8. You'll need four per window and one per seam between plywood sheets if using more than one sheet per window.

Keep Equipment Safe

Home office equipment — computers, printers, etc. — as well as other electronics and prized rugs and furniture should be protected before a hurricane approaches.

You also need to find a safe place for jewelry, irreplaceable documents and family photographs.

Here are some things you should do:

Make sure your electronic equipment is insured. However, some homeowner policies cover computers only if they are for personal use. People who run a business from home need supplemental insurance.

Back up your work on additional discs and/ or tapes and store them in a safe deposit box.

As the storm approaches, unplug all electronic equipment. Of course, you will want to keep one TV set working as long as there is power. A battery TV set is an ideal backup. Be sure to have extra batteries on hand.

Save the boxes the office equipment comes in. Pack the equipment, wrap the boxes in plastic (small boxes can fit into trash bags) and place on a high shelf in a closet.

Power Surges

After the storm, power surges may

occur, affecting sensitive equipment such as computers. Power crews can identify equipment problems prior to restoration so voltage problems don't occur. After Andrew, the over-voltage situations were extremely limited and the duration not long enough to damage normal equipment.

FPL encourages customers to consider surge protection. There are inexpensive protectors for individual pieces of equipment, such as VCRs/TVs, or electricians can install whole-house protection, the preferred method.

Personal property, such as jewelry and important documents, should be placed in a safe deposit box. If you cannot afford a box or do not have time to acquire one as a storm approaches, put your precious items in a watertight container and place it in the safest room in the house — the bathroom.

Save Family Photos

Losing family photographs is tragic. One way to safeguard such irreplaceable memories is to store the negatives in a safe deposit box. They don't take up much space and the cool, dry atmosphere is ideal. Should you lose family photographs, you can have new prints made from the protected negatives. Before a hurricane, you can safeguard photographs with plastic and move them to a place in the house likely to survive wind and rain.

Precious books should be wrapped in plastic and placed on a closet shelf.

Small collectibles and treasured knick-knacks should be packed in boxes as if for a move, and stored in a closet.

If your home is in a flood area, protect furniture by moving it to the highest, driest place in the house if possible. You also can elevate furniture on cement blocks, bricks or pieces of scrap wood to protect it from flooding. Stack smaller pieces of furniture on top of tables and sofas. For further protection, top your stacked furniture with tarps or Visqueen in case the roof develops leaks.

Oriental rugs should be rolled up, wrapped in white sheets, then in plastic, and placed in a closet.

Paintings too large to remove from the wall should be covered with plastic film (Visqueen). Pull the plastic to the back of the painting and secure with masking tape. Small paintings should be removed, wrapped in plastic and stored in a closet.

The same procedure can be followed with sculpture — wrap the large pieces in plastic, wrap and store small pieces in a closet.

Bring patio furniture, garden tools and garbage cans indoors.

Put Away: Oriental rugs should be rolled up and wrapped in white sheets and plastic, then put in a closet.

Gloria Wattley

"We were out of power for more than a week while everyone else on our block had power because a sea grape tree fell across our power lines. This year, we are going to make sure all of our trees are pruned properly."

Robert Moehling,
owner of Robert is Here
fruit stand, at entrance
to Everglades National
Park.

*"The first thing I did
after the hurricane, even
before we started to
rebuild, was to order hurricane shutters. We didn't
have shutters before
because I didn't want to
spend the dimes on them.
If we had put shutters up,
we would not have had
much damage."*

Acorn

Tree Selection And Care

Trees, if well chosen, will set the tone of your landscape, impart character, distinction, and add value to your property. The "well chosen" part is tricky. To get there, you have to determine a number of things, including what you want your trees to provide.

Do you want them to shade your house and reduce your energy bill? Provide you with oranges, mangos or some other fruit? Color your landscape at particular times of the year or all year round? Screen an unsightly view or provide privacy? Establish some wildlife habitat and a native setting?

How can you have all of these things and still have trees remain safe in a storm? Whittle down your choice by looking closely at several factors including space for ample development of roots and canopy, soil conditions, suitability (cold and drought tolerance), tree selection at the nursery and tree planting and care. All of these factors influence the health and safety of your trees.

Spreading Up And Out

How much space can you give to your trees? Trees in groupings can be planted relatively close so they develop an overall canopy. Specimen trees, selected to be solitary and singularly attractive in the garden, require space enough to stand alone. If you want shade from one live oak, do you have enough room to allow its natural

Live Oak
Quercas virginiana

A sturdy shade tree, the live oak is drought tolerant and provides food and shelter for wildlife.

spread to develop in the future? Do you know that spread could one day reach 100 feet, with the top of the canopy going to 70 feet?

Oh, you're right, it will take many years for your oak to get that big, but that's another consideration: the trees you plant, given care, may last for generations. So select wisely. Consult tree references, visit parks, botanical gardens, drive around and take notes in your neighborhood.

Watch Those Roots

Tree roots extend out about three times the height of the tree, so providing ample root room is important. In addition, as lots grow smaller, it's generally more difficult to find space enough for large 60-foot shade trees. Several smaller trees grouped together may be more in scale.

In general, smaller trees, trees that had been pruned and trees with a good form did better in Hurricane Andrew, yet even some small trees proved brittle.   The sabal palm, pygmy date palm, thatch and silver palms all did well. Gumbo-limbos, live oaks and royal palms withstood the storm pretty well, shedding limbs or fronds rather than toppling (not in the ground zero area, where winds gusted to 200 miles an hour), while damage to black olives and mahoganies was variable, depending on the condition of the tree. Avocados broke up, while mangos held up. Lime trees in South Dade were yanked from the ground.

Sea Grapes Hold The Wind

Sea grapes, orchid trees, yellow tabebuias went over or cracked, even though these are generally smaller trees. The sea grapes can be quite dense and act as sails, catching the full force of wind, particularly when planted in a group. Yet,

Royal Palm
Roystonea species
Wind-resistant royal palms shed older fronds during hurricanes. Young leaves at the tip soon emerge.

Sabal Palm

Sabal palmetto

The state tree of Florida, the cabbage palmetto, or sabal palm, is wind and drought resistant.

many South Dade residents believe the abundance of trees around their homes actually shielded their house from physical damage.

Tree roots with room to take hold did in fact hold up in the hurricane better than those too close to streets, sidewalks, buildings.

Soil. In selecting your tree, soil is a major consideration. The rocky and sandy soils of South Florida generally are alkaline, with a few pockets of acid sand near the coast, muck near the Everglades.

Very alkaline soils and very acid soils tie up micronutrients needed by plants, making them unavailable for plant growth, flower and fruit production. That means you have to keep an eye on your trees for signs of nutrient deficiencies, such as yellowing leaves or smaller growth, and provide micronutrients when they're in short supply. Plants not adapted to alkaline soils may require two or three foliar applications of micronutrients annually. It's best to routinely use a fertilizer that contains these micronutrients, or minor elements as they're often called. Plants

weakened from nutrient deficiencies will be more vulnerable to disease and insect damage as well as storm damage.

In addition to being alkaline or acid, soils also are characterized by drainage, fast or slow. Sand is extremely fast-draining; rock less so; mulch often retains too much moisture and becomes soggy. Organic materials, such as compost and peat moss, can improve water-holding capacity of sandy and rocky soils. But too much can discourage roots from extending beyond into poor soils and so discouraging adequate anchoring. So if you opt to improve your soils, don't add more than 30 percent amendments and add it over a large area, not just the planting hole.

Vulnerable To Rot

Generally, you can grow moisture-loving plants in drier areas more successfully than vice versa. Bald cypress, for instance, will grow outside a swampy, wet area, but it won't develop breathing roots called knees and it won't be as big and lovely as in the watery or even lakeside setting.

A tree from a rockland hammock, such as a paradise tree or wild tamarind, cannot sit in water many weeks and live. Citrus and avocado trees are especially vulnerable to rot from standing in water.

The Broward County Commission's Public Service Department, Agriculture Division and IFAS have jointly published a pamphlet called *Ornamental Plants for Landscaping Poorly Drained Areas.* Among plants able to withstand a week of flooding on a regular basis are Australian tree fern, bald cypress, banana, coastal plain willow, dahoon holly, Guiana chestnut, java plum, lady palm and dwarf lady palm, mahoe, mahogany, needle and pygmy date palms, sabal palm, satinleaf,

Southern red cedar, red bay, royal palm and wax myrtle.

Both sandy and rocky soils benefit from mulching to help retain moisture and increase fertility. When planting in soils over hardpan or compacted fill where drainage is poor, as in western Broward County, you can use trees and shrubs mentioned above, add soil amendments over a large area, or plant on a small berm of sand and muck (60 to 70 percent sand). Eventually, tree and shrub roots can work their way through densely packed fill, but they'll have a better chance of surviving the first few years given an extra boost.

Salt. If you are close to the bay, salt breezes are a consideration. The coastal hammock plants generally are tolerant of some salt air, including live oak, paradise tree, lancewood, buttonwood, gumbo-limbo, satinleaf, piegon plum, sea grape and Jamaica dogwood. Pines generally don't tolerate salt well, while cabbage palms do well anywhere.

Temperature. Coastal areas are warmer than inland locations, so cold tolerance also should be factored in. It's often 10 degrees colder a few miles inland, and in winter that can spell the difference between freezing or not. Tropical trees, such as some fruit trees, won't tolerate freezing weather. Even trees in the Florida Keys and the tropical areas of southernmost Florida, such as Geiger and wild tamarind, lose leaves in cold.

Brittleness. Some trees are beautiful but brittle. Keeping them pruned within restricted bounds should be built into your maintenance program if you plant them, and storm damage can result if you don't.

Earleaf acacia, silk oak, eucalyptus, avocado, African tulip tree, woman's tongue and umbrella trees are considered dangerous without the right pruning. These trees broke up readily in Hurricane Andrew. Do you want to buy into the trouble and expense? Avocados may be worth the trouble. Shallow-rooted trees, such as seaside mahoe, Australian pine and woman's tongue, are likely to topple over in storms.

Drought Tolerance. Most of our rainfall occurs over about five months, from June through October. The other months may see two or three inches of rainfall; they may see none; they may see quite· a lot. Our trees, then, have to withstand a wide range of moisture conditions once established.

Drought-Tolerant Trees

Among the trees that are drought tolerant, consider these: sweet acacia, allspice, pitch apple, rose apple, blolly, buttonwood, calabash, camphor, Jamaica caper, Guiana chestnut, citrus, coral tree, coffee colubrina, copperpod or yellow poinciana, crawbood, crape myrtle, Jamaica dogwood, yellow elder, fiddlewood, frangipani, Geiger, golden shower, cattley guava, gumbo-limbo, horseradish tree, black ironwood, jacaranda, Jerusalem thorn, joewood, southern juniper, kopsia, kumquat, lignum vitae, loquat, macadamia nut, southern magnolia, milkbark, millettia, mimusops, red mulberry, live oak, black olive, orchid trees, paradise tree, pigeon plum, South Florida slash pine, red silk-cotton, royal poinciana, sapodilla, soapberry, soursop, stoppers, strongbark, tabebuia, tamarind, wild tamarind, wax myrtle, wild cinnamon, wild dilly, wild lime.

Energy Conservation. Not only will drought-tolerant trees save water resources, if you place them wisely in the

Jack Wattley

"I went out and bought a generator after the storm and probably paid more than I should have. Installing the generator had to be done very carefully. They can be dangerous when done incorrectly."

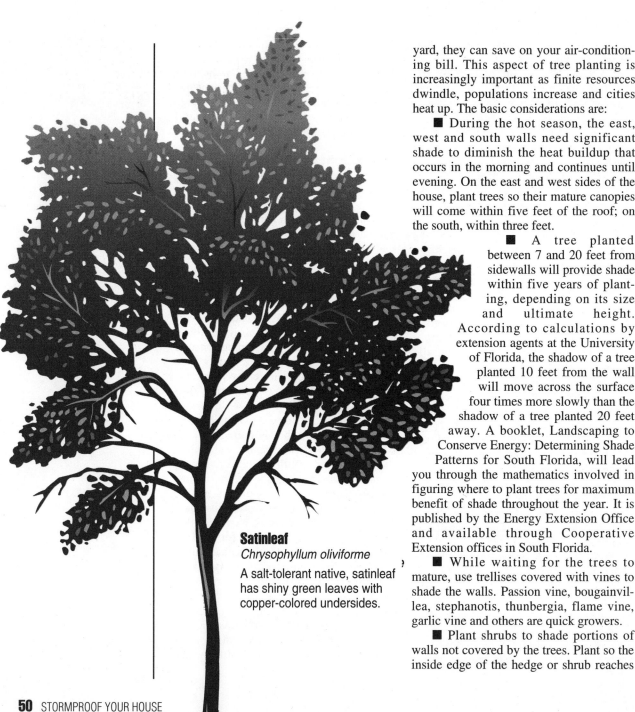

Satinleaf
Chrysophyllum oliviforme

A salt-tolerant native, satinleaf has shiny green leaves with copper-colored undersides.

yard, they can save on your air-conditioning bill. This aspect of tree planting is increasingly important as finite resources dwindle, populations increase and cities heat up. The basic considerations are:

■ During the hot season, the east, west and south walls need significant shade to diminish the heat buildup that occurs in the morning and continues until evening. On the east and west sides of the house, plant trees so their mature canopies will come within five feet of the roof; on the south, within three feet.

■ A tree planted between 7 and 20 feet from sidewalls will provide shade within five years of planting, depending on its size and ultimate height. According to calculations by extension agents at the University of Florida, the shadow of a tree planted 10 feet from the wall will move across the surface four times more slowly than the shadow of a tree planted 20 feet away. A booklet, Landscaping to Conserve Energy: Determining Shade Patterns for South Florida, will lead you through the mathematics involved in figuring where to plant trees for maximum benefit of shade throughout the year. It is published by the Energy Extension Office and available through Cooperative Extension offices in South Florida.

■ While waiting for the trees to mature, use trellises covered with vines to shade the walls. Passion vine, bougainvillea, stephanotis, thunbergia, flame vine, garlic vine and others are quick growers.

■ Plant shrubs to shade portions of walls not covered by the trees. Plant so the inside edge of the hedge or shrub reaches within a foot or two of the wall. This will create an air pocket, moderate wall temperatures and still allow air movement.

■ Plant trees or shrubs to shade the air-conditioning unit outside. Plant them so that in five years, their canopies will shade the compressor and the adjacent area during the morning and afternoons for the entire cooling season.

By planting the perimeter of your yard with a sturdy palette of native trees or trees that need no supplemental irrigation, by mulching beneath these and by keeping the amount of lawn to a minimum, your energy savings further increase. Mulching reduces the need for heavy fertilization, which in turn reduces the need for water.

Group plants of similar water needs together so you can efficiently irrigate them when they need it without wasting water on others. If you want to grow heliconias, impatiens (in winter), blue sage, Chinese hat plant or other shrubs and ground covers that need water, keep them in one area of the yard, closer to the house so the irrigation system can reach them without difficulty.

How To Buy A Tree

What do you look for when shopping for trees? A strong central leader (unless you are buying a multistemmed tree such as wax myrtle, sea grape or ligustrum); strong scaffold branches that create a framework of large branches to support smaller lateral ones. The trunk should be free of wounds, mutilated branches; bark firmly attached.

Do not accept root-bound trees. This can only lead to trouble. Unless corrected early, circling roots can eventually girdle a tree, cutting off water and nutrient flow on a side of the tree, weakening its hold in the

soil. Many trees that toppled in Hurricane Andrew had girdling, circling roots.

Look for a full, evenly distributed canopy, uniformly shaped. A lopsided tree will only be trouble. When taking your tree home, don't put the top down on the convertible and let the tree stick up in the air. This will pull water reserves out of the young tree. Cover the canopy; if possible, lay the tree on its side in the trunk, drive home slowly.

How To Plant

Dig a hole as deep as the container and three to five times the size of your new tree's rootball. Trees grow roots at remarkably fast rates — 5 to 7, even 10 feet a year in all directions. By digging a hole that's very wide, you will loosen soil into which these roots will grow in the first year.

If you amend the soil, adding composted manure or peat, remember no more than 30 percent amendment to the backfilled soil. If the planting hole is too rich, roots will stay there.

When backfilling around the rootball, use the hose to water in the soil so there are no air pockets left around the rootball. Then mulch over the whole area to a depth of two or three inches, making sure the mulch does not touch the bark of the tree to increase chances of fungus disease.

It takes about five or six months for each inch of trunk diameter for a tree to become established in the landscape. Water requirements are believed to be quite high during the establishment period, usually six months to two years. Ideally, you need to add supplemental water if you plant at the beginning of the rainy season. The whole idea is to keep the root zone moist until the tree is established, weaning

Charles Roberts

"Yeah, we are preparing. We just ordered $5,700 shutters. My wife ordered them. She said she wouldn't go through another season without them."

Kent Little

"I didn't even put up shutters but after seeing the damage with Andrew, I think I will. I just used duct tape on the windows. I haven't bought shutters yet; I'll probably go the plywood route. Most likely, I'll wait until the last minute like everyone else in Miami."

the tree to natural rainfall. Apply three gallons of water for each inch of trunk diameter daily for one to three months, then every other day and finally every three to four days. Adjust this according to rain. Roots will be growing outward during this period at the rate of about an inch or more each week, so enlarge the area you water.

Uprooted: Generally, smaller trees and ones that had been pruned did better in Hurricane Andrew than others. Among the trees that fared well were sabal palms, pygmy date palms, thatch and silver palms.

PRUNING TREES

Prune trees to maintain natural form and allow wind to flow through branches. Thin branches **before** hurricane season – high winds can turn a brush pile into destructive missiles.

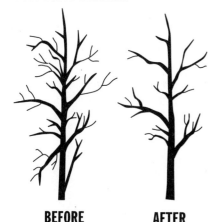

BEFORE   **AFTER**

A mature tree with crossed and broken branches should be cleaned up and thinned to scaffold branches to encourage strength and balance.

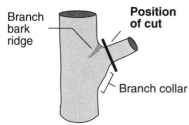

Branch bark ridge

Position of cut

Branch collar

When removing lateral branches, cut at an angle beyond the branch collar. Look for a raised area where the branch attaches to the trunk, and cut at an angle as shown. This will allow the tree to produce wound wood over the cut and recover more quickly.

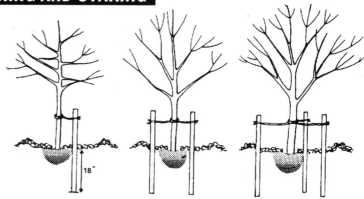

STAKING SMALL TREES

Trees with a trunk diameter of less than 2 inches can be anchored with a single 2-inch by 2-inch wooden stake 36 inches tall. Trees with a 2- to 3-inch diameter require two or three stakes sunk 18 inches into the soil.

STAKING LARGER TREES

Trees with a 4-inch or larger diameter at chest height should be guyed with three or four wires or cables run through rubber hose, spaced six to eight feet from the base of the tree. Mark guy wires and stakes with bright flags or other material to prevent accidents.

SOURCES: *Selecting and Planting Trees and Shrubs* by D.L. Ingram, R.J. Black and E.F. Gilman, University of Florida Cooperative Extension Service.

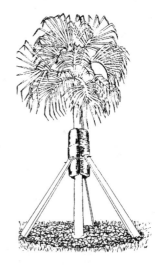

STAKING PALMS

When staking large palms, use padding or padded boards and nail wooden supports into the padding, not the palm trunk. Wrap boards with burlap and fasten these to the trunk with wire or metal straps.

CHAPTER 3

Getting Supplies

It's easier to shop when skies are sunny — buy only what you need. Consider other sources of power and water.

Last-Minute Preparations

It's the heart of Hurricane Season. Trouble percolates. A tropical storm has burgeoned into a hurricane hundreds of miles out to sea. Your morning paper warns that the storm's projected track threatens your community, possibly in three days.

You know you already should have made many of the preparations listed below — but you didn't. So, here's a timetable of things you still can do before it arrives.

Day 1

7 a.m. Start worrying.

7:05 a.m. Ease worrying, begin planning. Assess status of storm preparations. Know where you'll go if required to evacuate.

8 a.m. At work or home, listen to storm updates from now on.

Noon Fill car's gas tank, other cans if using a generator.

12:15 p.m. Refill pending prescriptions early.

3 p.m. Buy plywood or other home-protection supplies while available.

5 p.m. Buy emergency stocks such as canned food, drinks, batteries, camping supplies, manual can opener before stores get swamped.

8 p.m. Put important papers in safe, portable container.

9 p.m. Hurricane watch issued.

Day 2

8 a.m. Trim and take to the dump branches that could damage home.

9 a.m. Bring in outdoor objects, furniture that could fly.

11 a.m. Secure boat on trailer, or move to safe harbor.

1 p.m. Re-top gas tank, if needed.

7:30 p.m. Hurricane warning issued.

8:30 p.m. Gather clothing, blankets, toiletries, flashlights, radio.

Day 3

7 a.m. Put shutters, window protection in place.

11 a.m. Store extra water in jugs, cleaned bathtubs.

11:30 a.m. Don't waste time with elaborate last-minute shopping expedition; do make sure you have essentials.

Noon Move to shelter if you're in evacuation zone or prepare safe room.

7:45 p.m. Hurricane moves ashore. Stay inside. Listen to the radio.

9:15 p.m. Don't be lured out into danger by storm's quiet eye. Wait for all-clear message.

Last-Minute Rush: As the storm approaches, buy emergency provisions such as canned food, drinks, batteries and camping supplies. Remember to fill your car's gas tank because pumps may not be working once the electricity goes out.

Alicia Carras

"My family has always teased me because I have been stocking up for a hurricane for years. I have this massive 'canteen' with every kind of canned good, dog bones, toilet paper, batteries. Everything. It's very well stocked. Well I got my sweet revenge this year when my family came over for every meal and ate out of my canteen. They even borrowed stuff like candles and batteries. Showed them!"

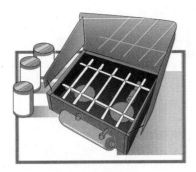

No-Electricity Oven

The reusable Girl Scout charcoal oven is a method of baking without using electricity. **Do not use it indoors.**

This oven, made of a cardboard box and aluminum foil, can be used to bake cookies, meat loaf, cobblers, shallow casserole dishes — even turkeys, anything that can be cooked at temperatures of 300 to 325 degrees.

Use an empty liquor carton that still has the lid attached on at least one side. Line the inside of the box and lid with foil. Cut cardboard pieces the size of each side, wrap them with foil on all sides, then line the inside of the oven with the pieces. Each side should now contain alternating layers of cardboard and foil, ending inside with the third foil layer.

Place the box on the ground with the lid opening up toward the sky.

Light five or six pieces of charcoal. (One piece of charcoal puts out about 50 degrees of heat Fahrenheit.) Do not use any more charcoal than that, or the box could burn. Place hot coals on the bottom of the oven.

Set your pan atop four empty tomato paste or small juice cans. You may add more charcoal, if needed, as the original charcoal burns out. Have water handy in case of fire.

Shopping, Cooking Tips

Stock your shelves with hurricane equipment and supplies well in advance. Once a hurricane watch is posted, you'll have too many other preparations to want to stand in long lines at the hardware and grocery stores.

Plan for a seven-day supply of nonperishable food, keeping in mind variety and ease of preparation.

The most important tool you'll use will be a manually operated, nonelectric can opener.

If the storm doesn't hit, save your supplies for the next scare. Once hurricane season is over, you can eat your canned goods or donate them to a holiday food drive. Most canned foods have a shelf life of a year or two, so it's a good idea to replenish your supplies yearly.

Here are some shopping and cooking tips:

You need a gallon of water per person per day. Don't count on last year's supply, either. Most plastic-bottled waters should be drunk within a year. Stock up on canned fruit and vegetable juices, seltzer and soft drinks.

To store water in the bathtub, sponge the tub with a solution of liquid bleach and water, caulk the drain to make it watertight and fill the tub. You can use this water for washing and cleaning. A bucketful will flush the toilet if municipal pipes fail.

Also, freeze water in plastic containers. If electricity fails, store them in the refrigerator to help keep food cold.

You won't want to use your bottled water for dishwashing, so get plastic or paper plates, knives, forks and spoons, napkins, cups and garbage bags. You also need toilet paper and pre-moistened towelettes. Consider heavy-duty aluminum foil for cooking on a grill.

Stock up on emergency lights, candles and matches and oil for hurricane lanterns, if you have them. Each family member should have a flashlight. Buy flashlight bulbs and batteries, which you also will need for radios, portable televisions and portable lamps. Have a fire extinguisher handy in case candles are knocked over.

Stock up on Sterno for cooking inside, or, for cooking outside after the storm, fuel for camp stoves and charcoal or gas for grills. If you have a fireplace, many foods can be cooked on skewers or wrapped in foil and cooked. But don't cook indoors with your charcoal grill or fuel-burning camp stove, even in the fireplace. The fumes are dangerous.

First-Aid Kit

Put together a first-aid kit. It should contain three rolls of gauze bandages, antiseptic ointment or spray for cuts, burn ointment or spray, ammonia inhalants, adhesive tape, scissors and tweezers. Also, make sure you have an adequate supply of prescription medication.

If you have a baby, small children or are on a restricted diet, shop accordingly. Don't forget diapers, baby food, medications and formula. Buy small toys to keep babies and children occupied.

Keep your family's size in mind. Try to buy sizes of food that you can use in one meal. Many canned foods deteriorate rapidly once opened.

For milk, chose evaporated, dry powder or the relatively recent arrival, aseptically packaged milk, which is real milk, treated at high temperatures and storable at room temperature.

Don't go into a cooking frenzy and prepare a bunch of food that you plan to keep in a cooler and eat over the next few days. Dangerous bacteria thrive under such conditions. Most emphatically, don't hard boil a dozen eggs and plan to store them at room temperature. That's an invitation to disaster. Odds are, you won't have a good way to heat foods, so don't count on instant soup and such. Buy what you can stand to eat at room temperature.

So Much To Eat

Think beyond tuna: Canned chicken, ham and other meats as well as canned beans will provide protein and variety. So will canned, ready-cooked noodles and spaghetti sauce.

Lunch-box size or individual cans of applesauce, puddings and the like will do you well. So will raisins and dried fruits. No-cook instant pudding can be mixed with shelf-stable milk for dessert. Now is the time for small packages of processed cheese foods (e.g., Velveeta) and cheese in a squirt can. Also, consider apple butter, peanut butter, jams and such.

Bananas, oranges, grapefruits, apples and other fruits will be fine at room temperature for a few days and can give a diet of mostly canned goods a needed blast of freshness.

Onions, fresh garlic and vinegar all keep fine at room temperature and can make canned tuna or beans palatable.

Close The Door

As the storm approaches, keep the refrigerator and freezer doors closed and turn the temperature control to the coldest setting. If the power goes off, the refrigerator will keep food up to 24 hours and the freezer up to 48 hours.

After the storm, mosquitoes are likely to be swarming. Lay in a supply of spray and citronella candles. Consider Avon's

Billy Williams

"If people did nothing else, they should go out and get a battery-powered radio, several flashlights and remember to never hook up a generator to the box. If they did those three things, they'd be OK."

SUPPLIES YOU WILL NEED

HOUSEWARES

Although you may have many of the things on this list, be aware that you will need enough to last several days.

❏ Plastic trash bags with ties, and large sealable plastic bags.

❏ Film. Buy enough for "before" and "after" pictures.

❏ Matches, preferably stick matches that can be struck on a rough surface.

❏ Paper towels, plates, cups and plastic utensils.

❏ Chlorine bleach (plain), tincture of iodine or water-purification tablets.

❏ Personal hygiene supplies and toilet paper.

❏ Clean, empty containers for storing drinking water.

❏ Ice chests.

❏ Pet supplies, such as cat litter, a scooper and, if necessary, prescription pet medication to last several days.

HARDWARE

If you already have these supplies, now would be a good time to be sure they are still usable.

❏ Silicone caulking for bathtub drains. Silicone caulk will not affect the taste of water and cleans up easily. Just use a thick bead around the seams and it will pull away cleanly when dry.

❏ Many cans of "canned heat" (Sterno®, etc.) and folding stove. It takes a lot of Sterno® to heat a little food. Do not heat food indoors with charcoal.

❏ Duct tape has numerous uses including taping windows.

❏ Lightweight fire extinguishers.

❏ A battery-operated radio with extra batteries.

❏ Battery-operated lanterns and flashlights with extra batteries and bulbs. Candles, kerosene lights or live flames can cause fires and severe burns. If you must use candles, do not light any more than you need and never leave one burning unattended.

❏ A manual can opener and puncture-type can key.

❏ Oven mitts for handling heated cans of food and Sterno®.

HURRICANE FOOD LIST

Buy supplies in plastic containers when possible. They are lighter and less fragile. If the storm is severe expect to be without electricity for about two weeks. Remember that cans of foods must be punctured before heating.

❏ Special diet needs and prescription medicines.

❏ Canned foods like vegetables, soups, fish, meats, fruits and fruit juice.

❏ Peanut butter and jelly.

❏ Bread, crackers, cookies, other baked goods.

❏ Evaporated nonfat or whole milk.

❏ Dried fruits.

❏ Cereal.

❏ Cheese and cheese spreads.

❏ Nuts.

❏ Instant drinks (coffee, tea, etc.).

❏ Pet foods.

MISCELLANEOUS

❏ A first-aid book and supplies including alcohol, salve for burns, aspirin, adhesive tape and bandages, cotton balls, cough and diarrhea medicine and the like.

❏ Mosquito repellent.

❏ A wind-up clock.

❏ Plenty of absorbent towels and rags.

❏ An air horn. This is a container of compressed air and a horn mechanism on top available at any marine supply store. It makes a loud blast that can attract attention for great distances.

Skin So Soft, too, as an insect repellent.

When cleaning up outdoors, you'll need sun screen. Also have on hand a clothesline and clothespins to dry things out and a mop and a bucket or two.

Buy a can of lime to sterilize garbage in case sanitation pick-up is slow returning to your area. Baking soda can deodorize the refrigerator, freezer and ice chests.

Keep all your receipts of items you buy after the storm before power is restored. Your insurance may cover the cost of emergency food and ice.

One Day's Menu

Breakfast: Cereal with shelf-stable milk. Banana or orange. Bread, rice cake or crackers. Fruit juice, milk or water. Coffee if you can heat water.

Lunch: Salad of canned beans (chick peas, white beans and red beans), sliced onion, oil, vinegar and dried herbs. Whole wheat crackers. An apple. A piece of hard cheese. Juice or soft drink.

Dinner: Canned chunk chicken tossed with black olives, chopped onion or garlic, Dijon mustard, oil and vinegar. Fruit salad (made from fresh fruits or by combining canned; give a splash of orange juice if you wish or stir in canned or instant pudding). Bread, crackers or roll.

Danielle Schechterman

"I was told to come home by many concerned friends and relatives. I was totally naive to any of the comments on the possible destruction and damage of Hurricane Andrew. My advice: Go home and don't think twice or second guess any natural force."

Making Meals: With some spices and a little ingenuity, you can turn long-lasting canned goods into tasty, filling meals.

Robert Sierra

"If I could tell people to do one thing it would be to take a first-aid class and keep supplies at home. I almost lost my fingers. I was trying to hold this door shut and pieces of the roof were being ripped away. I could look up and see trailers flying like airplanes overhead. We were stranded at our house — blocked by fallen trees and debris. The police couldn't come and we couldn't get help. If we had owned a first-aid kit I would have been able to take care of it myself."

Water Tanks

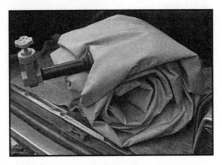

Handy Holder: Collapsible storage tanks come in six sizes.

Hurricane victims in need of water can store as much as 1,340 gallons at a time in collapsible water-storage tanks.

The tanks, called Kolaps-A-Tanks, are made of coated, industrial-strength, reinforced nylon and can be stored in closets and unfolded and filled when needed. They are approved by the Food and Drug Administration.

The tanks are produced by Burch Manufacturing Co. and sold by Domestic Water-Works, Cave Junction, Ore.

Six sizes are available, starting at 73 gallons. The lightest tanks weigh 11 pounds, and the largest 64 pounds. Prices range from $259 to $795.

For information, call Domestic Water-Works at (503) 592-3615 days or evenings, or write the company at P.O. Box 809MH, Cave Junction, Ore. 97523. The tanks can be shipped overnight or by two-day air.

Generators

If your area is going to be without power for a long time after a hurricane, you may want to invest in a generator. Your homeowner's insurance may pay for it.

Generators are fueled by gas, the same kind you use in your car; by natural gas piped into your home; or by propane gas, which also fuels barbecue grills.

Generators, which resemble small automobile engines, are started by pulling a cord, similar to cranking a lawn mower. Some expensive models have starter buttons or keys. Veteran generator users say the latter is much easier to use, especially for people who may not have the strength to pull a choke cord. Wear gardening gloves to avoid burns when pulling the choke cord.

If you can afford it, get a generator with a large gas tank. A two-gallon tank has to be filled every two hours; a 15-gallon tank will run all night.

The wattage a generator produces determines how many appliances you can run. Wattage ranges from 750, which will run a light and a fan, but not much more, up to 8,000 watts, which will practically power an entire house except for central air conditioning. To run a refrigerator, you'll need a generator that produces 3,000, 4,000 or 5,000 watts.

Homeowners who tried to run too many appliances on a generator after Hurricane Andrew risked wearing out the appliance motors or ruining the compressors. Wattage above 4,000 can run appliances that require 110 or 220 volts, such as stoves and washing machines.

It's important to remember that a gen-

Chris Schloss

"Make sure you have all the prescription medicine you'll need. You may not be able to get to a pharmacy right away."

Power Source: Fueled by gas, generators can run appliances and fans. You'll need a generator that produces 3,000, 4,000 or 5,000 watts to run a refrigerator.

erator requires proper care and maintenance. The oil must be checked every time you add fuel. Most generators get 150 hours of running time before the oil must be changed. If the oil isn't changed, the rings could blow.

The operation is also dangerous. Generators should be placed in a well-ventilated area, preferably outdoors. Gasoline-powered generators produce carbon monoxide, which can be deadly in an enclosed area.

Be extremely careful when transporting gas in gas cans from the station to your home — the fuel is combustible. If, when filling the tank, you spill gas on a hot muffler, it might flame.

Additional Tips

■ Connect an appliance to the generator via a heavy-gauge extension cord. Don't run all the appliances at once; alternate them. For example, run the refrigerator eight hours and it should stay cold for another 20 without the generator.

■ Avoid connecting the generator to the home's main wiring at the circuit breaker. Improper use of generators can cause electricity to flow backward into the power lines, endangering FPL workers or possibly even neighbors served by the same power line.

■ Homeowners who used generators after Andrew advise wearing old clothes because spills of gas and oil are inevitable. They said their "generator clothes" had to be discarded eventually.

■ Generators are noisy. Be prepared for neighbors' complaints.

■ When electric power is turned on, it will not affect the appliances connected to the generator because the power is restored to the house, not to individual appliances.

■ When electricity returns, empty the gas from your generator before storing.

CHAPTER 4

Protect Pet, Car, Boat

Andrew's lessons reveal many choices, but your safety matters most.

Saving The Animals

Right now is the best time to make preparations for your pets' safety during a storm.

Dr. Ronald Stone, Miami veterinarian who headed Florida Hurricane Pet Aid after Hurricane Andrew, said the best thing you can do is prepare ahead; the worst is to think of it in the middle of the storm.

Here are some options for pet care.

If you live in an evacuation area, you'll be asked to leave your pets behind because emergency shelters won't accept them. So find out if your veterinarian has boarding facilities or other arrangements for boarding animals, and make an appointment to inspect the kennel. Inquire about staff and security.

If you are satisfied that the kennel or vet's facilities are safe, make an appointment ahead of time to board your dog or cat. Many vets already have standing reservations for the next storm, so don't delay.

Motels For Pets

Call the American Automobile Association or hotel/ motel association and

Care and Comfort: Make sure planning for pets includes supplies at home or arrangements to board them. If you must leave town, call the American Automobile Association or a hotel association and ask for a list of facilities that allow pets

ask for a list of hotels and motels that will take pets if you plan on leaving town. If you must evacuate, you'll know where to stop instead of setting out blindly only to be told no.

Check every year to make sure the kennel or veterinarian still can take your pet or pets, and keep a contingency plan written down and kept where you'll remember it.

Buy a pet carrier or taxi that is slightly larger than you actually need so when you take your animal to a pet hospital, it has a cage in which to stay should the shelter or hospital be full. Take along an extra bag of dry food with your pet's name on it, an extra bottle of water and any medicine your pet needs.

A Safe Room

If you must leave your animals at home, put them in the most secure room in the house, along with dry food and water. You can buy devices that contain several days' supply of food or water, or you can leave out a large bucket of water.

When the storm approaches, make sure your dogs and cats are wearing collars with identification and rabies tags. Stone said hundreds of volunteers who worked with escaped pets after Hurricane Andrew had no idea of how to track owners. Counting horses, pigs, chickens and the rest, there were several thousand animals on the loose.

If you keep your animals at home,

John Meyerholz

"I would stay with Tyrone [his dog, Tyrone Power]. He has been in the family for a long time.

If we had some idea ahead of time we might try to drive north, but you never know if it is going to hit. That guy who makes all of those predictions might be wrong for once."

make sure you have a sufficient supply of any medication for them, just as you do for yourself. Assemble vaccination histories of your animals in case a situation arises calling for immunization of all dogs or cats.

Stock up on your animal's favorite food (so there won't be yet another disruption in routine), water and dishes. Have a familiar blanket on hand so it can be a security blanket for the animal.

For horses, provide food and water. Dr. Sidney Nusbaum, Boynton Beach vet on the board of the American Academy of Veterinarian Disaster Medicine, says it's better to allow the animal to remain loose within a fenced area than tied in a barn that could be crushed in the storm. Their reflex is to turn their back to the wind and hunker down, Nusbaum said. And put a halter loosely on the horse with some identification on it.

Giving tranquilizers to your animal is something you must discuss on an individual basis with your veterinarian.

Treat Injuries

Finally, get a pamphlet on emergency care of pets, and read up on what you might need to treat wounds, shock or other injuries. The pamphlets are usually at your vet's office.

Fancy fish owners with valuable aquariums may want to purchase a small generator for running the air pump if electricity goes out or buy a battery-operated aerator.

As a result of Hurricane Andrew, the American Veterinary Medical Association is putting together guidelines on dealing with natural disasters. When complete, the information will be available to vets and pet owners alike, so keep in touch with your veterinarian and get a copy when it's ready.

Keeping Cars Safe

How can you protect your car during a hurricane?

The first thing you can do if you have a garage full of "stuff," is to clean it out so you can park your car in it when a storm approaches.

Back your car against the garage door to give the door additional support.

If you have a carport, park your car in it before the storm. It will provide some protection from rain and flying debris.

Families with multiple cars may not have garage space for all. Park the newest, most valuable vehicles in the garage.

If you have neither garage nor carport, park your car as close to your house as possible. At least one side of it will be protected from flying debris. Try to anticipate the direction of the wind and place your car where it will be most protected.

A canvas cover (the kind you can buy for around $200 at an automobile dealer or parts store) may protect your car's finish from scratches and nicks during a storm, but the wind will likely tear off the cover.

A canvas or vinyl car awning provides no protection during a hurricane. You should unlace the cover, fold it up and take it into the house. Awning poles cemented in place offer no resistance to the wind and should not be standing after the storm.

Public Garage

Consider checking your car into a public parking garage for the duration of the storm (that is, if you have transportation home). Two-car families could park one in a public garage and keep one for transportation. Beware that you might not be able to retrieve your car immediately after the hurricane, should there be flooding or if roads are closed because of fallen trees

Shore Up Door: Reinforce garage doors with steel or wood trusses. Garage doors on older homes might need to be braced with a vertical mullion locked in place in the center line of the door.

Annie Moore,
Age 18

"I would stay, but I think I would bring my horse inside the house this time."

or poles.

There is usually little glass in parking garages, but if the sides are open to the elements, debris and water could damage your car.

If electricity is off after the storm, disengage your electronic garage door and open it manually. All garage door openers have an emergency disconnect — a small cord hanging from the mechanism at the top of the door. Pull the cord and it disengages the electric motor from the door.

Reinforce Garage Doors

Garage doors are required to be reinforced with steel or 2-by-4 wood trusses (also called U-bars) to meet the Dade County Building Code. Garage doors that failed during Hurricane Andrew often did because they weren't installed properly. If the jamb provided by the builder was not done properly, the garage door frame couldn't hold.

If your garage door was installed before the mid-1970s when the wind load code became effective in Dade County, you might brace the door with a vertical mullion locked in place in the center line of the garage door. The mullion is simply an aluminum I-beam custom tailored to fit the garage. Any metal shop can fabricate one so that it attaches to the concrete tie beam over the door, approximately on the center line of the door, and to the cement floor. You are simply connecting one concrete structure to another with the aluminum I-beam.

Most new garage doors are made of galvanized steel that complies with the wind load code. Some are backed with wood, which makes the door more flexible should an object hit it during a storm. Such doors need no extra bracing.

Pamela Schloss

"Don't start preparing for the hurricane the day before it's supposed to hit. Start early putting papers together, buying canned goods and water, and make sure you have enough baby food. We had 11 10-day-old puppies when the hurricane hit. I had to go out and buy every single can of goat's milk I could find to make sure they had enough to eat. It's just like stocking up for a baby."

Plan For Your Boat

The lessons to be learned by boaters from Hurricane Andrew are many.

But few lessons should be as clear as this: Going somewhere is better than going nowhere.

Raul de la Torre, the dock master at Miami's three city-operated marinas, said 138 of 250 boats left at Dinner Key sank during the storm. In contrast, he said only eight of 250 vessels that were moved elsewhere met the same fate.

"The difference in proportions is extraordinary," de la Torre said. "People know now that the chances of their boat being damaged are higher in a marina than somewhere else."

Seek Refuge

Both the city of Miami and Dade County, which operates six marinas, will continue to encourage boaters to seek refuge elsewhere and hold them liable for damages if any occur.

But marina managers elsewhere are taking a much harder stand and altering policies as a result of Andrew.

George Carter, director of the Riviera Beach Municipal Marina in Palm Beach County, allowed two boats to stay during last year's storm. He has since retained the services of a towing firm and will have vessels evicted in similar circumstances this year.

"We have revised our leases and notified owners that their boats will be cut loose if they refuse to do it themselves," Carter said. "Many people up here just don't understand the devastation that will occur."

The Lake Park Municipal Marina, also in Palm Beach County, promises to oust boaters when a hurricane draws near. Several vessels were permitted to remain last year.

"When you make somebody get out, you feel like you are being too rough on them but you really aren't," dock master Doug Stout said. "The reality is that people should think about hurricane plans for a long time."

Several boaters from Miami took their crafts all the way to Key West to escape Hurricane Andrew. But the same boats would be turned away now.

"We have decided not to allow anyone to stay here at all," said Patrick Conner, a dock master at the privately owned Galleon Marina. "In all honesty, we think a marina is not the best place for a boat to be in a hurricane."

Conner, who grew up on the hurricane-vulnerable Alabama coast, spent two days studying Andrew's destruction at Dinner Key.

"I could tell some people hadn't secured their boats properly, but I'm not sure it would have made any difference," he said. "The damage was amazing. I noticed a 100-foot section of dock exactly like ours blown 200 yards up the beach."

Reserve Dock Space

The destruction caused to boats at coastal marinas should teach boaters to seek refuge in inland waterways and reserve dock space at private facilities in more protected areas.

"Taking a boat up an inland waterway is always better than leaving it at a marina near the ocean," said Ernie Braatz, manager of the Damage Avoidance Program for the Boat Owners Association of the United States, the country's largest group of recreational vessel-owners. "And the

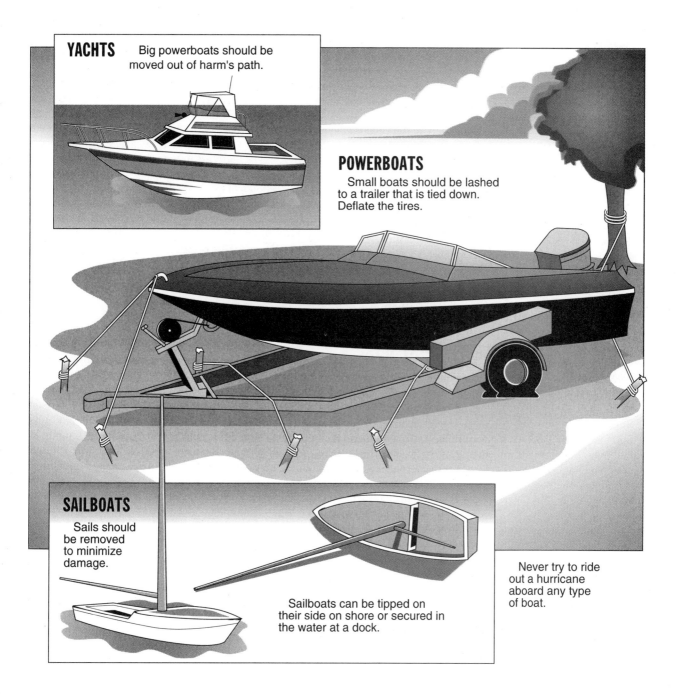

YACHTS Big powerboats should be moved out of harm's path.

POWERBOATS

Small boats should be lashed to a trailer that is tied down. Deflate the tires.

SAILBOATS

Sails should be removed to minimize damage.

Sailboats can be tipped on their side on shore or secured in the water at a dock.

Never try to ride out a hurricane aboard any type of boat.

Marinas

Broward County

City of Fort Lauderdale facilities:

Birch-Las Olas Docks, 85 Las Olas Cir., Fort Lauderdale; 468-1593; 38 wet slips.

Cooley's Landing, 450 SW Seventh Ave., Fort Lauderdale; 468-1626; 32 wet slips.

New River Docks, 2 S. New River Dr. East, Fort Lauderdale; 761-5423; 112 slips.

Hollywood Municipal Marina, 700 Polk St., Hollywood; 921-3035; 55 wet slips.

Fort Lauderdale City Docks, 2 S. New River Dr. East; 761-5423; 190 wet slips at nine facilities, average 45 feet.

further inland you go, the less the chance of damage there is.''

Damage incurred by boaters who tied their vessels up carelessly in inland waterways should also act as a deterrent in the future. Losses could have been minimized if boats were better secured.

''I was amazed at the extent of damage up the Coral Gables Waterway,'' Braatz said. ''Many large boats sank and were smashed against docks. But there was no excuse for it.

''People were simply overconfident. If their boats had been tied with heavy enough lines, and had been secured with cross lines, they probably would have survived quite well.

''What you need is a coordinated effort, not a situation where every man works for himself.''

More Boat Tips

Advance Planning

■ Check your lease or storage rental agreement. Some marinas require a boat to be removed when a hurricane approaches.

■ Check the condition of your boat's hull, deck hardware, rigging, ground tackle, machinery and electronics. Absentee owners should arrange for a supervised inspection in preparation for hurricane season. This includes making sure batteries are charged, bilge pumps are operable and equipment is secured.

■ Develop a detailed plan to secure your vessel in a marina, move it to an area out of the storm's path or take it to a previously identified hurricane refuge.

■ Make arrangements with the marina, other boat owners or designate someone to move and protect your boat.

■ Ask other boaters, the Coast Guard or Florida Marine Patrol to suggest a protected body of water to take your boat in a storm.

■ Know the route, navigation requirements at different tides and restrictions like bridges and channels if plans call for moving a vessel inland.

■ Rehearse the plan, including an actual visit to the alternate dock or anchoring or mooring location. Make arrangements well ahead if renting dock space.

■ Make sure your insurance policy is current. Understand coverages and exclusions and your responsibilities as a vessel owner.

■ Be sure your tow vehicle is capable of moving the boat. The tires, bearings and axles should be in good condition. The same is true of a trailer.

■ Consolidate all records, including insurance policies, a recent photo of your vessel, boat registration, equipment inventory, lease agreement with the marina or storage area and telephone numbers of appropriate marine authorities and keep them in your possession.

■ Maintain an inventory of items to be removed and left on board. Mark items of value so they can be identified in a hurry. Keep copies of the list on board and at home.

■ Before a hurricane threatens, analyze how you will remove valuable equipment from the boat and how long it will take.

■ Purchase necessary materials like additional lengths of mooring lines, anchors, chafing gear, fenders, fender boards and screw anchors ahead of time.

■ Inspect the vessel's deck hardware. Many boats suffer from having cleats that are inadequate, a critical problem when a second set of larger-diameter lines are used with existing ones. If necessary, add more and larger cleats before the season. Check stress points like cleats and winches to be sure they have substantial backing plates and make sure they are secured with bolts of adequate size.

■ Make sure docks and seawalls are sound, mooring cleats are secure and pilings are in good condition at wet slips.

■ Coordinate safety and mooring arrangement plans with other vessel owners and neighbors if you are going to dock in a residential area.

As The Storm Approaches

■ Seal windows, doors, hatches, lockers, portholes and vents with duct tape. Shut sea cocks and plug through-hull fittings, including sink drains. Bang a plug into the engine's exhaust pipe — but remember to remove the plug later before starting the engine.

■ Cover instrument gauges with duct tape and other built-in equipment with plastic bags fastened by the existing mounting screws.

■ Strip all loose gear: antennas, Bimini tops, booms, canvas covers, curtains, deck boxes, dinghies, extra lines, fighting chairs, life rings, outriggers, portable davits, running rigging and sails. Remove gear from cabinets in the cabin and secure cabinet doors.

■ Take home all marine electronics.

■ Remove sails from sailboats, particularly roller furling headsails, which are almost sure to unfurl in high winds. Run halyards to the masthead and secure them with a single line led to the rail to minimize damage to the mast.

■ Attach chafing gear to mooring lines because they tend to break when rubbed against a boat or dock. Old canvas or garden hose can be used to cover the lines.

Trailered Boats

■ If you don't have room for both, leave your boat, and not your car, in the garage because a boat is lighter and more vulnerable to high winds. Put the boat and trailer where they will get the best protection from wind and debris if it's not practical to store them in a garage.

■ Let air out of the trailer tires and block the wheels. Increase the weight of lighter outboard boats by leaving the drain plug in and adding water with a garden hose. This has the added advantage of giving you emergency water if service is interrupted by the hurricane. Place wood blocks between the trailer's frame and springs to support the added weight. Remove the drain plug on an inboard/outboard engine so it won't be damaged by flooding.

■ Secure the trailer with heavy lines to fixed objects and try to pick a location that allows you to secure it from all four directions. Strip loose gear — anchors, antennas, Bimini tops, booms, canvas covers, portable davits, dinghies, electronics, life rings and running rigging — and then lash the boat to the trailer.

Boats And Davits On Lifts

■ Remove boats from backyard davits or lifts and store them ashore if possible because water can rise higher than the boat can be raised.

■ Remove the drain plug so the weight of accumulated rainwater will not collapse the lift if a boat must be left on one.

■ Tie the boat securely to its lifting machinery to prevent the boat from drifting away.

Dade County

City-operated marinas
Dinner Key Marina, 3400 Pan American Dr., Coconut Grove; 579-6980; 582 wet slips.

Miamarina at Bayside, 401 Biscayne Blvd., Miami; 579-6955; 200 wet slips.

Watson Island, MacArthur Causeway on Watson Island; 579-6955; 37 wet slips to 60 feet.

County-operated marinas

Black Point, 24775 SW 87th Ave., Homestead; 258-4092; 176 wet slips, 40 dry storage slips.

Crandon Park, 4000 Crandon Blvd., Key Biscayne; 361-1281; 222 wet slips, 128 dry storage spaces, 60 anchorage moorings.

Haulover Marine Center, 15000 Collins Ave., Miami Beach; 945-3934; 44 wet slips, 300 dry storage spaces.

Homestead Bayfront Park, 9698 N. Canal Dr., Homestead; 247-1543; 173 wet slips, 40 dry storage spaces.

Matheson Hammock, 9610 Old Cutler Rd., Coral Gables; 665-5475; 252 wet slips, 71 dry storage spaces.

Pelican Harbor, 1275 NE 79th St., Miami; 754-9330; 98 wet slips.

Monroe County

Key West Municipal Marina, 1801 Roosevelt Blvd., Key West; 292-8167; 150 wet slips.

■ Plug exhaust outlets and strip the boat.

Nontrailered Boats

■ Store your boat ashore if it can be removed from the water and will be sheltered from rising water, falling trees and flying debris. Larger boats that have low freeboards, such as high-performance powerboats, are safer ashore. The same is true of sailboats with deep keels.

■ Move a vessel at least 48 to 72 hours before a hurricane is estimated to strike the area.

■ Make sure fuel tanks are full, fuel filters are clean, batteries are charged, bilges are clean, cockpit drains are free and clear, firefighting equipment is in good order and lifesaving equipment is in good condition and readily accessible before a boat is moved.

■ Ask a marina to remove your boat's drain plugs if it is being kept in dry storage on an elevated rack. The weight of rainwater trapped in a boat can cause a rack to collapse if the shelter's roof is even partially blown off. Drain gasoline tanks to reduce the chances of fire before a vessel is put in dry storage.

Boats Remaining In A Marina

■ Plan to move your boat to a hurricane harbor or out of harm's way in event of a storm. Marinas are not considered safe.

■ Double all lines to help secure a boat if there is absolutely nowhere else to go. Rig crossing spring lines fore and aft and tie lines as far down on a piling as possible to reduce stress on the pilings.

■ Leave enough slack in all lines to enable the vessel to rise and fall with the tide or storm surge. Make sure lines will not slip off pilings.

■ Cover all lines to prevent chafing by wrapping them with tape, rags and hoses. Install fenders to protect the boat from banging against boats, piers and pilings.

■ Make sure batteries are fully charged to ensure their capacity to run bilge pumps for the duration of a storm. Cut off all devices consuming electricity other than bilge pumps.

■ Do not stay aboard. When winds are blowing 100 miles per hour, tides are surging and visibility is two or three feet, there is little one can do to save a boat.

Boats At Mooring Or Anchorage

■ Make sure the mooring block or anchors are heavy enough to hold your vessel. Use anchor weights well above what you would normally use.

■ Reduce chances of the boat dragging by using a permanent mooring — a mushroom anchor and chain — with two storm anchors. Using the anchors with the mooring increases holding power and decreases the room a boat will need to swing. A third storm anchor can be used instead of the mooring.

■ Use sufficient chain to eliminate dragging and chafing while the vessel rises and falls with the storm surge and tide.

■ Do not extend an anchor off the stern. A vessel needs to swing with storm winds, surge and tide.

■ Give anchor and mooring lines enough range to withstand rising tides and storm surge.

■ The best mooring location for a vessel to ride out a storm is in the center of a canal or narrow river where at least doubled mooring lines can be secured to both shores, port and starboard, fore and aft.

■ Do not remain on your vessel.

If Caught On Board

■ Throttle down to a speed that will keep you headed into wind and waves if caught in open water. Deep water produces swells, as contrasted to stronger wave action in shallow water. Use a sea anchor if well offshore.

■ Stay away from windows.

■ Open windshields on the bridge to minimize injuries from blown-out glass.

■ Wear life jackets at all times.

■ Tie a safety line to yourself and attach it to the vessel.

■ Turn off anything that could produce a flame.

■ Stay tuned to weather radio channels.

■ Be aware of all vessels in the vicinity and give wide berth.

■ File a float plan. The marine telephone operator can file for you but you must pre-register. Letting an operator know where you are will make communications with shore much easier.

After A Hurricane

■ Get to your boat quickly.

■ Notify your insurance agent as quickly as possible if the vessel is damaged.

■ Secure the boat as best as possible. Seal broken windows, take home wet carpets and drapes for cleaning and take home anything remaining that could be stolen.

■ File a report with local police if there has been any theft or vandalism or loss other than that related to the storm. Obtain a copy of the incident report number and copy of the incident report if possible to substantiate an insurance claim or revenue loss.

■ Hire a competent marine mechanic

to flush and preserve your engine if it has been submerged even briefly. Leave the boat submerged until a mechanic is available, however, because the engine can be permanently damaged if exposed to air without being flushed and preserved.

■ Arrange for pumps to be put aboard if the boat is taking on water and have it removed to dry land. Most insurance policies cover raising and hauling out a boat, but it is best to contact your agent first.

■ Promptly list all parts of the boat believed to be damaged to speed handling of repairs and processing of insurance claims. Take photos and get written estimates. Get your insurance company's approval before starting repairs.

■ Appoint someone in writing to act on your behalf if repair and salvage decisions need to be made.

Security: Pets cannot communicate, so you need to think ahead to prevent injuries.

Palm Beach County

Lake Park Municipal Marina, 105 Lakeshore Dr., Lake Park 33403; (407) 842-2724; 224 wet slips to 48 feet.
  Palm Beach Municipal Marina, 500 Australian Avenue Docks, Palm Beach; (407) 838-5463:
  Australian Dock (407) 838-5463, 24 slips.
  Brazilian Dock, (407) 838-5464, 31 slips.
  Peruvian Dock, (407) 838-5463, 23 slips.
  Riviera Beach Municipal Marina, 200 E. 13th St., Riviera Beach; (407) 842-7806; 145 slips, 201 dry storage spaces.

CHAPTER 5

Where To Go

Safety may be found in shelters, inside your house, apartment or condo. You might even hit the road.

Stock Medical Supplies

All it takes is a little forethought to make hurricane preparations easier for people with special physical and psychological needs. Here are some tips based on the Hurricane Andrew experience:

Anyone who needs medication should have at least a two-week supply in a hurricane kit. This is especially important for people with conditions such as heart problems, high blood pressure, depression and epilepsy. And, don't forget birth control pills.

Diabetics should have a cool place for their insulin supply, although it will keep safely for a month at room temperature (85 degrees). Diabetics also should monitor their blood sugar more often during the emergency, because stress and irregular eating could affect it. Have hard candy or juice available for reversing insulin reactions.

Stockpile a two-week supply of disposable diapers for a baby or incontinent adult. These were the first essentials to run out after Andrew.

Seeking Safety: People in evacuation areas may go to shelters or leave the community for safer spots. If heading to a shelter, bring an adequate supply of medication, a first-aid kit, games and toys for the children, dry clothes and plastic trash bags.

Baby Formula

Bottle-fed babies need single-serve formula that doesn't require refrigeration, available in stores. Also stockpile baby bottles of sterile water for infants.

Talk before hurricane season with friends or relatives who are frail, seriously ill or handicapped, or unable to function well without electricity. Many health officials now recommend that they leave the area altogether if a hurricane is approaching.

Where will they go? How will they get there? Do they need your help in evacuating? Do they have copies of medical records or a summary of current treatments to take with them? Remember: A person who is relatively independent in good times can be needy in an emergency.

Ask doctors ahead of time how to maintain contact in an emergency. Answering services sometimes have back-up phone numbers.

Elderly residents of high-rises should not stay there. Even inland, power failures after the storm could trap them there indefinitely.

Pregnancy

Are you a high-risk pregnancy patient or in your last month of pregnancy? If so, ask your doctor which hospital you should go to as a hurricane approaches. Make arrangements ahead of time for your children. Hospitals that take in pregnant patients during a hurricane won't allow

Rosa Mercado

"If another one heads our way, I am packing up and leaving. We probably will. But where to?"

children or spouses to come along.

Insect repellent is especially important for the young, the old and people who are already weakened by sickness.

Decide which room your family will go into if the worst happens. Essentials for the room include shoes for everyone (so you won't step on nails in debris later), and a rugged, waterproof container with medical and property insurance papers, immunization records and medical records of anyone with special needs. Get a container big enough to hold a few cherished mementos, which will be comforting later if the house is destroyed.

Letting children help with the storm preparations will allow them to talk about their fears and feel more in control. Answer their questions honestly but without dramatizing what could lie ahead. Give lots of verbal reassurance, hugs and cuddles.

Save your children from worrying about their beloved pets by planning ahead. Make sure vaccinations are up to date before the season, and consider tattooing the pet's torso for easy identification if you are separated.

If you live in a coastal area, take your pets along if you leave the area..

Shelters

If your storm planning includes a shelter, here are some hints from the Red Cross and people who stayed in shelters about what to take and what to expect:

First, a shelter is for people in an evacuation area who have no other place to go. You can't stay with friends or relatives, and it's too late to leave the area. Stay home until radio or television stations announce the shelter for your area is open.

Packing for a shelter, unlike a vacation, is for an uncertain amount of time. At shelters, you won't have access to amenities like washing machines, or perks like privacy.

Think about roughing it. Depending on the number of people who show up at a shelter, blankets may be in short supply. If you have a favorite pillow, bring it. Sleeping bags also are a good idea.

Pack For Shelters

Make sure to bring an adequate supply of medication you or your family requires. It's also a good idea to bring a first-aid kit and some children's aspirin. Shelters are confined areas, and germs can spread quickly.

Bring some games, toys or coloring books to help you and your children pass the hours. Choose carefully, and keep them to a minimum. Space at shelters is at a premium.

Bring pens, pencils and paper. You'll be receiving a steady flow of information from newspapers, radio and television. A notebook will help keep track of things you need to do.

Bring dry shoes and socks, especially for children. They will be out playing around the shelter and are bound to get wet feet. Clothing you've left at home may be wet when you return home.

Plastic trash bags, with ties, help minimize odors from dirty socks and clothes.

Valuables, like photographs or great-grandpa's watch, need to be considered carefully. It's best to store jewelry, stock certificates or other financial papers in a safe-deposit box before the storm. Photographs and other important papers, like insurance documents, should be kept near you. Remember, though, all departments of banks may not be open for business for several days following the storm.

Haven At Home: Small, interior room without windows may be the best place to ride out a storm at home. Fewer openings mean fewer chances for the winds to roar in, and the walls of smaller rooms tend to be more stiff.

Bryan, Marie Carpenter

"A central point in our rebuilding effort was the strengthening of our walk-in closet to with-stand the worst that nature has to offer. It's simple, relatively inexpensive and provides much peace-of-mind. Each of the existing aluminum studs in the walls around the closet were reinforced with wooden studs at right angles. The interior walls of the closet were then lined with 'tongue and groove' lumber. Likewise, tongue and groove boards were nailed above to produce the ceiling. The result is a very secure interior room made of interlocking lumber, which continues its normal use as a walk-in closet. The cost of material and labor was only $300-$400."

Bring a willingness to pitch in and help. Volunteers may be unable to get through due to downed trees and power lines.

Finally, bring your sense of humor. It will be sorely needed and greatly appreciated.

Safe Room

If you're riding out a storm at home, where's the safest place to be? An interior room without windows — like a bathroom. The reasons are structural and psychological. Any small, interior room without windows will offer more protection than a windowed, exterior room.

Windows can be shattered by a small pebble, if hurled by 100-mph-plus winds. Doors, especially those with glass insets, can be blown or sucked open. Fewer openings mean few opportunities for the winds.

Structurally, the walls of smaller rooms have less length, so they are more stiff.

To illustrate the point, think of a 2-by-8 piece of wood, suggests John Pistorino, a structural engineer and Metro-Dade consultant. It will flex more easily than a 2-by-4. In the same way, longer walls will flex more easily than shorter ones. And, because the walls are closer together, the roof "doesn't have to span so far," Pistorino said. "The smaller the space, the less apt that it's going to fly apart."

Interior rooms also offer the added protection of being surrounded by other walls, so they are shielded.

And, aside from structural reasons, a small, dark space just feels safer.

Tom Wattley

"I live in an apartment and basically made sure all the plants and patio furniture were inside and the furniture was away from any windows. I tried to board up as best I could and then I left and went to a friend's house to weather the storm."

Condos, Apartments

House or apartment renters would be wise to map out their plans with the landlord before hurricane season begins. Coordinating plans protects both parties' property and may avoid problems if, for example, a home is damaged by makeshift shutters put up by the tenant.

Apartment or condo dwellers need to take special precautions. Remember, elevators depend on electricity to run and in a severe storm, electricity may be out for days.

Planning Tips

■ Select a "hurricane czar" — someone who knows how to prepare for a hurricane and who will tell residents what precautions to take.

■ In large high-rises, designate a floor captain to report to the czar and be responsible for keeping track of the residents of that floor.

■ Assign drivers for residents with limited ability to get to the store for supplies.

■ Call a mandatory complex-wide meeting to discuss hurricane plans and distribute a list of suggested hurricane supplies. This would be a good time to appoint hurricane czar and captains.

■ Locate a safe area within the complex for residents to gather in case of emergencies. Tell residents to stay away from sliding glass doors and windows.

■ Locate all exit stairways, noting the exit nearest you. Count the number of steps from your door to the exit in case you have to do it in the dark.

■ Determine a location outside the building for family members and other residents to regroup in case evacuation becomes necessary.

■ Close and lock all windows, sliding glass doors and shutters. Secure patio doors to prevent them from being torn off, close curtains and move furniture away from windows.

■ Remove all loose items from the terrace or patio such as hanging plants, patio furniture, barbecue grills, and gardening supplies. Assign a group of residents the responsibility of preparing common areas in larger complexes.

■ Secure grounds by setting up guidelines for safety of cars and recreational equipment.

■ Establish a phone chain to ensure all residents are aware of approaching storm and any evacuation orders.

■ Make provisions for sheltering people who might be trapped when the evacuation routes are closed by the approaching storm.

Precautions: High-rise dwellers should close and lock all windows, sliding glass doors and shutters and secure patio doors to prevent them from being torn off. Take all loose items off the terrace or patio and move furniture away from windows. Residents at Saga Bay Apartment complex lost everything.

Elizabeth Ligon

"If you need a safe place for irreplaceable treasures, such as photo albums, books, paintings, important papers, put them in your empty appliances — washer, dryer, dishwasher, oven or microwave. I wish I had packed some dry clothes in plastic bags. If there is a next time, I will be sure to have a supply of large plastic bags for clothes, blankets, towels and to put over computers, lamps, TVs. Fill whole garbage cans with water to use for flushing toilets, bathing, washing clothes. Keep a set of tools with you during the storm. Be sure to take videos and photographs before the storm of every room and all sides of the house for insurance purposes. Then take pictures of everything after the storm."

Candace Style,
Age 10

"I would leave. I wouldn't want to go through that again. I talked to my family about it. When we leave, everyone else will be behind us because we'll be the first."

Corey Johnson,
Age 10

"I'm outta here. I'll go to Georgia with my family and I'll stay there the rest of my life if I have to. That hurricane was bad. I don't want to see one of those again."

Escape Plans, Routes

Here are four plans to follow when a hurricane threatens:

Plan A: If your home is safe and secure, stay there. Mobile homes and boats are not safe. Neither are areas that local officials designate evacuation areas. If you live in such an area and a member of your family is bedridden and requires constant care or, regardless of where you live, if a family member has electrical life-support equipment at home, call your local Red Cross chapter for special instructions.

Plan B: Make plans to stay with relatives or friends who live in safer areas and be sure their home is adequately prepared.

Plan C: Leave the area well ahead of time because of heavy traffic.

Plan D: Go to a Red Cross shelter as a last resort. Wait until shelter openings and locations are announced on local radio and TV broadcasts. Not all shelters may be opened. You must go as soon as possible. Don't expect luxury accommodations. Eat before you leave. Bring your own supplies but remember that pets, alcohol and firearms are forbidden.

Supplies Include

Snacks, canned food, milk and other beverages, a manually operated can opener and eating utensils. Take food that does not have to be cooked.

Medicine. If your medication must be refrigerated, take a small portable ice chest and ice.

A pillow and a blanket or a sleeping bag.

A battery-operated radio, a flashlight and extra batteries.

Water. Plan on one to two quarts of water per person per day.

Identification and valuable papers, including insurance papers. Keep all your valuables on your person at all times.

Toothbrush, toothpaste, deodorant and a change of clothing.

If you have a baby, don't forget baby food and diapers.

Cards, games and books.

Sightseeing: These drivers trying to see their homes near The Falls during Hurricane Andrew ran into dangerous conditions.

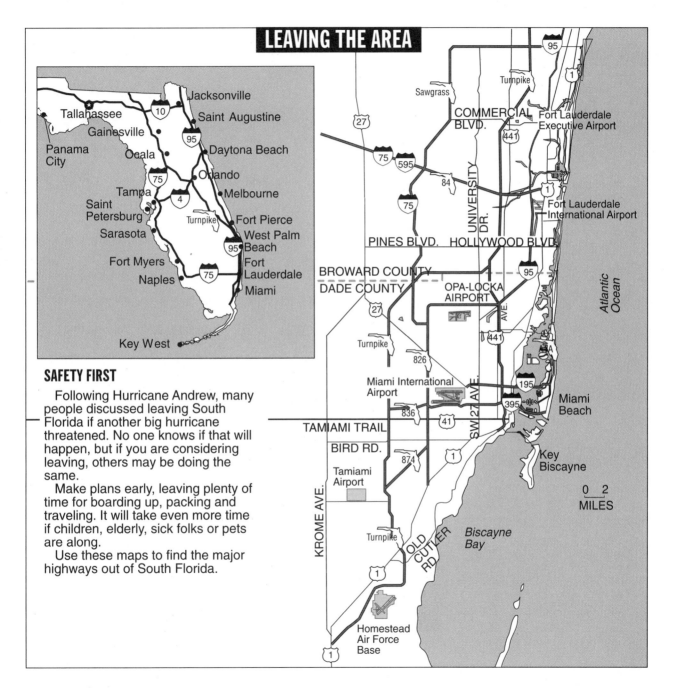

LEAVING THE AREA

SAFETY FIRST

Following Hurricane Andrew, many people discussed leaving South Florida if another big hurricane threatened. No one knows if that will happen, but if you are considering leaving, others may be doing the same.

Make plans early, leaving plenty of time for boarding up, packing and traveling. It will take even more time if children, elderly, sick folks or pets are along.

Use these maps to find the major highways out of South Florida.

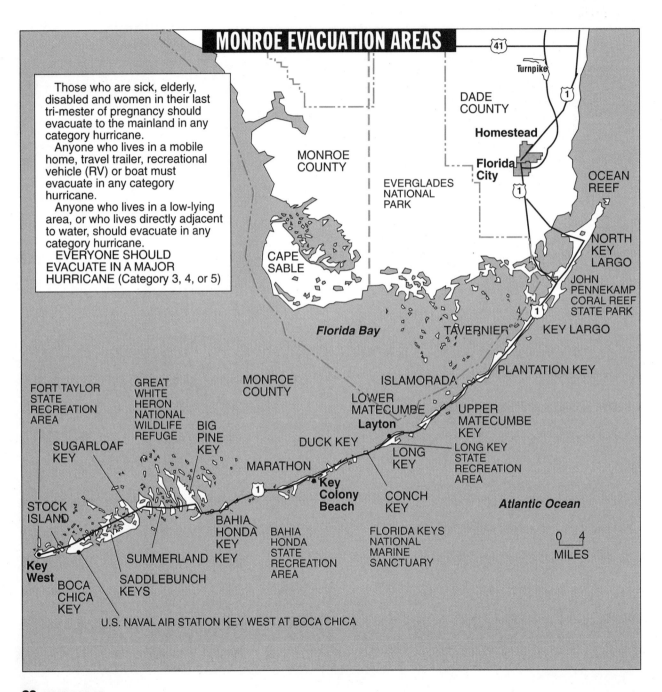

MONROE EVACUATION AREAS

Those who are sick, elderly, disabled and women in their last tri-mester of pregnancy should evacuate to the mainland in any category hurricane.

Anyone who lives in a mobile home, travel trailer, recreational vehicle (RV) or boat must evacuate in any category hurricane.

Anyone who lives in a low-lying area, or who lives directly adjacent to water, should evacuate in any category hurricane.

EVERYONE SHOULD EVACUATE IN A MAJOR HURRICANE (Category 3, 4, or 5)

Turnpike

DADE COUNTY

Homestead

Florida City

OCEAN REEF

MONROE COUNTY

EVERGLADES NATIONAL PARK

NORTH KEY LARGO

JOHN PENNEKAMP CORAL REEF STATE PARK

CAPE SABLE

KEY LARGO

Florida Bay

TAVERNIER

PLANTATION KEY

ISLAMORADA

MONROE COUNTY

LOWER MATECUMBE

UPPER MATECUMBE KEY

FORT TAYLOR STATE RECREATION AREA

GREAT WHITE HERON NATIONAL WILDLIFE REFUGE

Layton

LONG KEY STATE RECREATION AREA

SUGARLOAF KEY

BIG PINE KEY

DUCK KEY

LONG KEY

MARATHON

CONCH KEY

Atlantic Ocean

STOCK ISLAND

Key Colony Beach

Key West

BAHIA HONDA KEY KEY

BAHIA HONDA STATE RECREATION AREA

FLORIDA KEYS NATIONAL MARINE SANCTUARY

0   4
MILES

BOCA CHICA KEY

SUMMERLAND KEY

SADDLEBUNCH KEYS

U.S. NAVAL AIR STATION KEY WEST AT BOCA CHICA

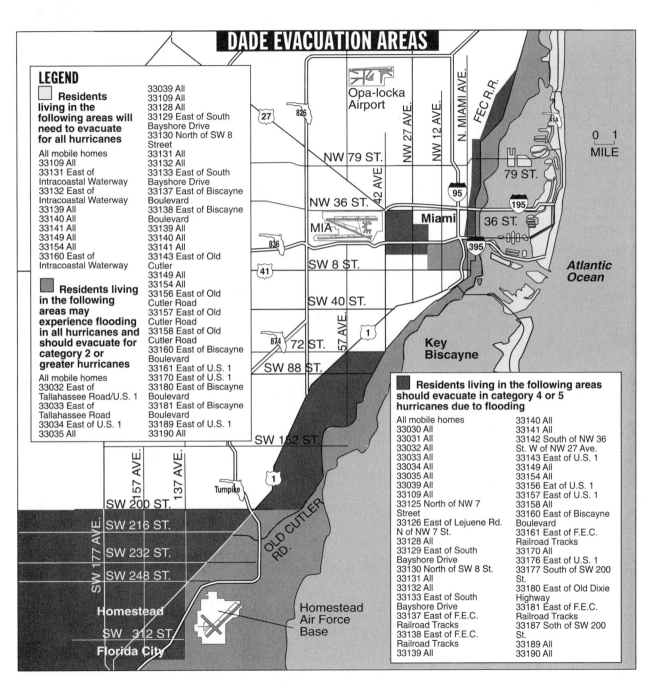

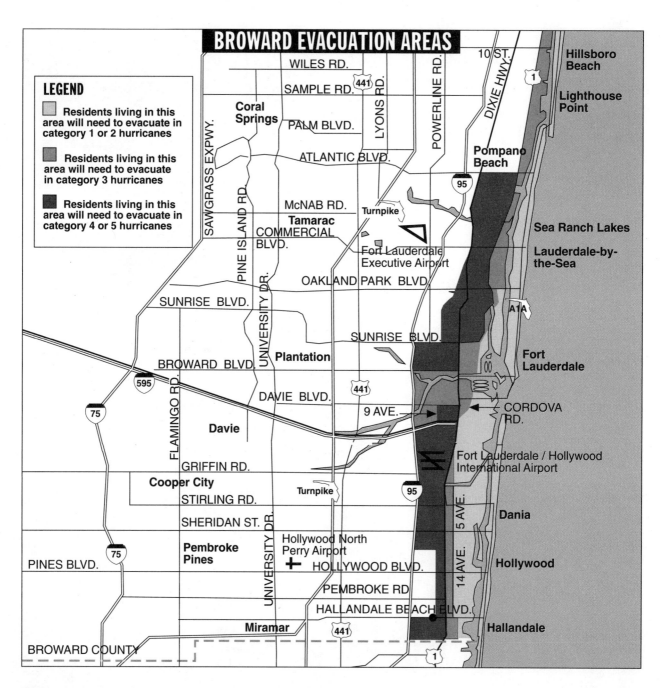

BROWARD EVACUATION AREAS

LEGEND

Residents living in this area will need to evacuate in category 1 or 2 hurricanes

Residents living in this area will need to evacuate in category 3 hurricanes

Residents living in this area will need to evacuate in category 4 or 5 hurricanes

WILES RD.

SAMPLE RD.

441

10 ST.

1

Hillsboro Beach

Lighthouse Point

Coral Springs

PALM BLVD.

LYONS RD.

POWERLINE RD.

DIXIE HWY.

ATLANTIC BLVD.

Pompano Beach

95

SAWGRASS EXPWY.

PINE ISLAND RD.

McNAB RD.

Turnpike

Sea Ranch Lakes

Tamarac

COMMERCIAL BLVD.

Fort Lauderdale Executive Airport

Lauderdale-by-the-Sea

UNIVERSITY DR.

OAKLAND PARK BLVD.

SUNRISE BLVD.

A1A

SUNRISE BLVD.

Fort Lauderdale

Plantation

BROWARD BLVD.

441

595

DAVIE BLVD.

75

9 AVE.

CORDOVA RD.

FLAMINGO RD.

Davie

Fort Lauderdale / Hollywood International Airport

GRIFFIN RD.

Cooper City

STIRLING RD.

Turnpike

95

5 AVE.

Dania

SHERIDAN ST.

UNIVERSITY DR.

Pembroke Pines

Hollywood North Perry Airport

75

PINES BLVD.

HOLLYWOOD BLVD.

14 AVE.

Hollywood

PEMBROKE RD.

HALLANDALE BEACH BLVD.

Miramar

441

Hallandale

BROWARD COUNTY

1

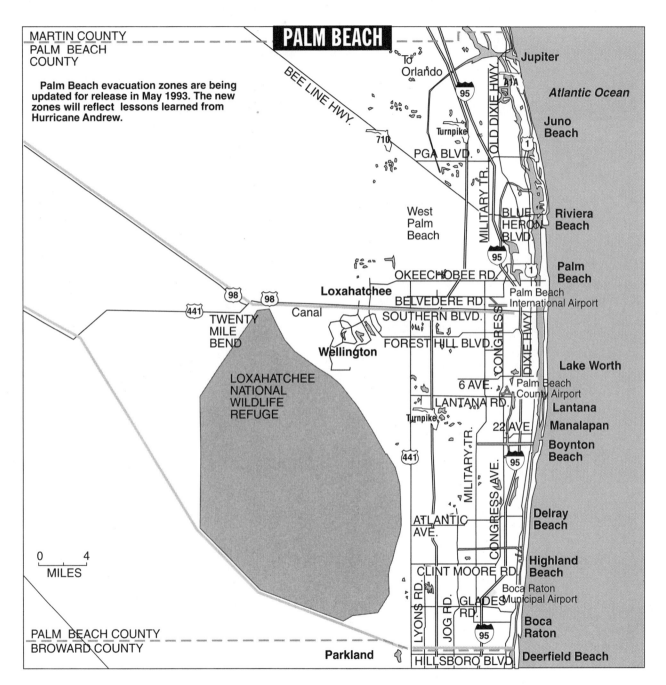

PALM BEACH

MARTIN COUNTY
PALM BEACH
COUNTY

Palm Beach evacuation zones are being updated for release in May 1993. The new zones will reflect lessons learned from Hurricane Andrew.

To Orlando

Jupiter

Atlantic Ocean

BEE LINE HWY.

Turnpike

710

PGA BLVD.

Juno Beach

OLD DIXIE HWY.

A1A

95

1

MILITARY TR.

West Palm Beach

BLUE HERON BLVD.

Riviera Beach

95

1

OKEECHOBEE RD.

Loxahatchee

Palm Beach

Palm Beach International Airport

98

98

441

TWENTY MILE BEND

Canal

BELVEDERE RD.

SOUTHERN BLVD.

CONGRESS

DIXIE HWY.

Wellington

FOREST HILL BLVD.

Lake Worth

LOXAHATCHEE NATIONAL WILDLIFE REFUGE

6 AVE.

Palm Beach County Airport

441

LANTANA RD.

Lantana

Turnpike

22 AVE.

Manalapan

MILITARY TR.

Boynton Beach

CONGRESS AVE.

95

Delray Beach

0   4
MILES

ATLANTIC AVE.

Highland Beach

CLINT MOORE RD.

LYONS RD.

JOG RD.

GLADES RD.

Boca Raton Municipal Airport

PALM BEACH COUNTY
BROWARD COUNTY

Boca Raton

95

Parkland

HILLSBORO BLVD.

Deerfield Beach

CHAPTER 6

Use Caution

The danger doesn't stop once the storm has passed. Be careful inside and out.

Don't Get Hurt

After the storm, common-sense rules should prevail. But be particularly careful when using motors — generators, chain saws, automobiles as well as devices that use electricity or produce heat or a flame.

Florida Power & Light warns that electricity produced by improperly installed generators can travel back through the lines and electrocute repair workers. Generators should be used only with an extension cord to the appliance you want to power. Make sure the wattage is the same — sending too much electricity can blow the condenser and ruin the appliance.

Cook with care. Do not burn charcoal or wood in the house or enclosed places. The chemical process for these fires produces carbon monoxide gas, which is odorless and highly toxic and can kill.

Also toxic are lighter fluids used to start fires. Before putting food on the grill, let the fluid burn off completely. Do not put food on a grill that has been doused with fluid and do not stand over grill, shoot fluid onto coals and cook food in

Obstacle Course: Drivers, riders and pedestrians should navigate debris-clogged streets carefully after a storm. Watch out for downed power lines, blown-down street signs and traffic signals. In the absence of traffic lights, treat all intersections like four-way stops.

fluid-induced flame.

Sterno, propane and natural gas can be burned indoors on a limited basis and in a well-ventilated area. Open a door or window for good measure when cooking with these fuels.

Always watch open flames and never put them near blowing curtains or billowy clothes. Never let children watch or carry candles or other fires and always keep fire extinguishers handy.

When working outside, remember: A chain saw is a dangerous tool in the hands of a novice. Even if you've used a chain saw in the past, be extra cautious. Knots in trees can cause chain saws to buck and fly back at arms or legs. Don't operate near cables, electrical wires or metal. Wear long-sleeved shirts, long pants, heavy boots and goggles to protect against flying wood chips.

If you must drive, be ready for impassable streets and blown-down street signs and traffic signals. Approach every intersection as if a speeding car were about to cross your path. In the absence of traffic signals, all intersections must be treated like a four-way stop.

Shirley Zieve

"1. Invest in a good bottle opener.

2. Get some heavy dropcloths and put them on all the furniture.

3. When rain is coming down on your chandelier, open an umbrella and put it upside down underneath.

4. To prevent odors in your refrigerator, put some vanilla on a cotton ball and put one on each shelf — including the freezer.

5. You can pick up the smallest piece of glass by using a wet cotton ball.

6. When the top of my dresser got wet, I put on Vaseline jelly and left it on for a few days. It left no water stain.

7. When there was no water, just drinking water, I wiped the sink with shaving cream.

8. Use alcohol to wash your hands. If you don't have alcohol, shaving cream will do.

9. When drawers are a little damp, put talcum powder in them."

Post-Hurricane Timeline

Based on what happened following Hurricane Andrew, here's what the days after a mighty hurricane might bring:

First Day

Electricity is mostly out. Perishables perish.

Field hospital opens.

Boil-water orders are issued.

Most government agencies are closed.

Traffic lights don't work.

Gasoline won't pump.

Red Cross and other relief organizations issue appeals for help.

With darkness, the first night of curfew.

Second Day

Looters are determined to profit. Police work 12-hour shifts.

Court appearances are canceled.

Ice is grabbed as quickly as it becomes available.

Some stores open. Shoppers snatch up things like diapers, baby food and batteries.

Truckers have difficulty finding stores; there are few street signs.

Traffic on major highways grows as those who fled the storm return.

Demand is high for tarpaulins, Visqueen, building supplies, ladders and spray paint. The latter for scrawling messages on remaining walls to insurance companies and trespassers.

Pay phones are set up.

Electricity partially restored.

Third Day

The volume of telephone calls almost overwhelms Southern Bell system.

Tractor-trailers loaded with building supplies hurtle by pickup trucks bearing ladders, laborers and license plates from miles away.

Fourth Day

Main streets are cleared of most debris; many secondary roads are still impassable.

Southern Bell sets up phone banks at Red Cross shelters. Public schools juggle schedules. Some will operate on split shifts.

Fifth Day

Local governments pass an emergency ordinance outlawing exorbitant pricing.

The toll-free number the state Department of Professional Regulation offers for consumers to check contractors' records is constantly busy.

Sixth Day

Fast food companies open mobile units, cooking and serving free food. Other restaurants also offer free food to hurricane victims.

Seventh Day

There is still no mail delivery in worst-hit areas. The Postal Service chooses pick-up sites.

Government offices begin operating. Some parks, facilities and libraries reopen.

Trash collection is sporadic; recycling doesn't exist.

The branches of many financial institutions are open; mobile units are in place at or near damaged branch offices.

Repairs are under way. People are falling off roofs.

Danger Signs

Danger remains even after the hurricane has passed and the all-clear is announced. Heed this advice:

Do not go out unless you have to. If you are in a shelter, wait until you are officially released. When you return home, drive carefully.

Roads and bridges may have been weakened and could collapse. Avoid trees, signs, buildings and other structures that appear damaged. Don't go sightseeing.

Stay away from disaster areas unless you are qualified to help. If you can't help, your presence will interfere with rescue and first-aid work. If you need medical care, seek it at a Red Cross disaster station or a hospital.

Avoid fallen or low-hanging wires and anything that is touching them. Stay away from puddles. They could be deceptively deep, contain hidden and dangerous debris or be electrified by fallen, live wires.

Stay away from river and canal banks. Weakened earth could collapse beneath you. Remember that high water will drive snakes, animals and insects to high ground, so be cautious and prepared.

If your home is damaged, enter with care. If you did not turn off electricity and gas before leaving, turn it off now. Don't light any matches if you neglected to turn off the gas. When turning off the electricity, wear rubber-soled shoes, rubber gloves, stand on a dry board and use a piece of wood, plastic or rubber to touch the switch handle.

Use your telephone only to report life-threatening hazards, such as live power lines, broken gas and water mains or overturned gas tanks.

If your power has been off, check frozen and refrigerated food for spoilage.

Be cautious about drinking water. Newspaper and radio reports will anounce when it is safe. Use bottled water in the meantime. Never use water from puddles or gathered from rainwater — and don't let pets drink water you wouldn't drink.

If your rugs are wet, pull them outside to dry in the sun. It will take several days. To avoid mildew, don't let the rugs remain in one spot the entire time.

If salt, sand, mud or sewage came into your home, move damaged items outside and rinse them with fresh water. If the water mains are broken and it's raining, let the rain do the job. If valuable papers got wet, put them in a pan of clear water, clean gently and spread on a table to dry.

To avoid warping wooden furniture, dry it outdoors out of direct sunlight. Remove drawers and other moving parts as soon as possible. If drawers are swollen shut, don't pry them open from the front. Remove the backing and push the drawers out.

If clothing and other fabrics are wet, separate to avoid running colors and mildew.

Do not use water-damaged electrical appliances until checked by a competent repair person.

List all damage to your home and other possessions. Insurance companies will send adjusters to damaged areas. Listen to radio and TV broadcasts to learn the location of disaster assistance centers, where those with damage claims or special needs will be able to file insurance claims or apply for government loans. Expect long lines.

Beware of profiteers, price-gougers and fly-by-night outfits. Deal with reputable firms for home repairs and items such as glass or lumber that you need to make your own repairs.

Re-Connection Woes

FPL cannot re-connect power to your house if the weatherhead, the equipment above and around your meter, is damaged.

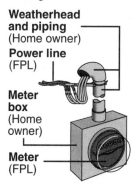

Weatherhead and piping (Home owner)

Power line (FPL)

Meter box (Home owner)

Meter (FPL)

■ **An electrician** should be called if you see any damage to the house connection, to the pipe that carries wires to the meter or to the metal box that surrounds the meter.

■ **If your neighbor** has a similar problem, consider making your request together.

■ **Visual inspection** should be done from the ground. Do not touch any electrical equipment or lines.

■ **If you are not sure** what is needed, FPL crews will be able to advise you.

Alissa Byrd,
Age 9

"Take your birds and pets into the closet with you, if you can, and put a mattress in front of the door. Put all the pictures of your friends into a box, and all the games and toys you want to save, and take the box with you."

Help Kids Adjust

After a hurricane, children mostly need comforting and security, experts say.

Don't be surprised if your 3-year-old sucks his thumb or clings tenaciously to your leg, if your third-grader wants a parent to tie her shoelaces, or if your 10-year-old insists on sleeping with Mommy and Daddy.

Children who are struggling show it in different ways. Some are hostile or withdrawn. Others cry at the wind or rain or have nightmares. They also crave attention and physical contact.

Don't Stifle Anger

Parents should not stifle their children's anger. Listen to it, redirect it if you can, and let little ones cry. Talk and play about the hurricane. On the other hand, don't use it as an excuse to let your kids do whatever they want. Appropriate discipline and setting boundaries are just as important now as ever.

Families need to re-establish their routines and sense of security as much as possible. If the family always said grace before eating, do so even if you're having to eat at an emergency site. If children have always enjoyed a story before bedtime, tell one.

Remember to take time for hugs, kisses and affectionate chats.

This is sometimes a challenge for parents, because they need help and comfort, too. Things are worse for kids whose parents are panicked because they transmit that fear to their children.

Parents should be on the lookout for children feeling that they are to blame for the hurricane, the experts say. They need to know what happened is nobody's fault.

But it's also important not to downplay the child's natural reactions. Tell them you understand they're scared and reassure them everyone was scared.

Adolescents need reassurance, too, but they can be difficult to reach because their insecurity comes out as anger and contentiousness.

Making a special effort to listen to adolescents and to let them participate in family discussions about the future can help. So can making sure they have a real role in rebuilding.

When children return to school, even formerly independent children may fear being separated from their parents. Reassure the child that school is a safe place, and that the child will be reunited with parents at the end of the day. Remind the child of all the good things that happened over the summer, and in school the previous year.

Tell the teacher if your child is having a hard time. Class discussions of the storm will help.

Kids' Activities

Journals, day books, diaries or logs can provide a means of expressing emotions and capturing experiences. They can also become lifelong records that provide memories and a window to the past. Sharing is important; the insights gained can alert parents and teachers to the unanswered questions and unresolved issues still concerning the writer.

Journals can take a number of forms: composition books, notebooks, scrapbooks, annotated photo albums, stapled sheets of paper, audio or video recordings. Memorabilia may include photos, receipts, roof shingles and any other mementos. Families might want to keep a common journal.

Get Started

Here are suggestions for getting started. If you have very young children, you can read the journal starters to them so they can draw pictures or dictate responses that reflect their ideas.

When I first knew the storm was coming. . .

To get ready for the storm, we. . .

I spent the hours during the storm. . .

The storm sounded like. . .

The scariest part of the night was. . .

When I walked outside after the storm, I saw. . .

The first thing we did was. . .

My neighborhood. . .

I knew I was safe when. . .

During the storm my pet. . .

The thing I'll miss the most. . .

Living without electricity, telephone, and/or water. . .

The weirdest meal I have eaten since the storm. . .

My favorite hurricane meal. . .

I really worried about. . .

My greatest loss is. . .

Things I did to help. . .

Something I've gained. . .

The most amazing thing I saw. . .

The hardest thing for me. . .

The nicest thing anyone has done for my family. . .

An important lesson I have learned. . .

I'll never forget. . .

Keith Culbertson,
Age 18

"We would get prepared a lot earlier. We would get more supplies and more water, for sure. I would also try and find a better place to leave my car. Actually, I'm glad we stayed, because we were able to save our house."

Time Out: Children need to be helped through the trauma a storm brings. Parents should let their little ones cry and not be afraid to talk about the hurricane. Make time for hugs, kisses and affectionate chats and re-establish as many routines as possible.

INSECT PESTS

These are some of the most common insect pests and how to get rid of them.

ANTS

Spray nests with insecticide or use ant bait--often boric acid with a sweetener--to stamp them out.

COCKROACHES

Spraying insecticides around the base of the house, using baits and clearing debris from around the structure will send most of these bugs scurrying away.

MOSQUITOES

Keep them out of the house by making sure screens and mosquito netting cover windows

Creepy, Crawly Critters

When their homes are destroyed by the winds and rain of a storm, critters do what many residents do — they move into whatever is left.

Ants march into whatever cracks, crevices or openings they can find and establish new nests. Rout them by finding the nests and destroying them.

Some nests, like those of fire ants, are huge mounds that are easily visible. Other ants like a bit more privacy.

Most black ant nests aren't out in the open, so use ant bait. Baits are carried back to the nest and kill the ants. Spraying kills only the critters the spray touches. The nest remains intact.

The same is true for the tiny, half-translucent Tapinoma ants. The extension service recommends using a boric acid-based bait with a sweetener to attract ants.

Mosquitoes and their eggs are not blown away by the gusts. The biters come out in force, and more hatch daily.

It's hard to avoid them. Cover any openings with screening. If screens or windows are missing, stretch screening or mosquito netting over the opening and fasten it with duct tape.

Some pests, particularly roaches, may stay outside for a while.

Roaches especially like piles of debris. As these are cleared away, the roaches will lose their food source and begin to look elsewhere. As with other pests, using bait is an effective way to control the population.

Spray the base of the house and part of the landscape with an insecticide such as Diazinon, Sevin or Dursban. This will help control pests, but will not totally eliminate them.

For heavy infestations, repeat once a week. Rain will wash away the insecticide and sunlight breaks down the chemical structure. For light infestations, a monthly spraying should be enough.

Piles of debris also attract other critters, notably snakes. According to the University of Florida's Institute of Food and Agricultural Sciences, the most common hiding places for snakes are inside houses and sheds, under debris and in garages.

Indoors, check under and behind appliances. If you find a snake, try to isolate it in a small area. If you're not sure whether a snake is poisonous, ask a wildlife conservation officer or the police department to remove it.

Outside, common sense is your best defense. Snakes like to sun themselves on fallen trees and other debris. When cleaning up, don't lift debris with your hands. Instead, lift it or turn it over with the handle of a rake or a board, then move it with your hands.

If you find a snake, step back and leave it alone. Snakes generally move slowly and won't strike immediately.

Good Riddance

Rats and mice also may become a problem. Traps or baits are the most effective ways to dispose of these pests.

Exposed wood surfaces, such as trusses, soffits or plywood sheets, will attract carpenter ants and termites as well as mildew and fungi. A product called Bora-Care will kill these. It's a boron-based product that is sprayed on unpainted wood. It is generally sold through pest-control operators.

FIX YOUR OWN PHONE?

Many homes won't have a working phone at all after a storm. Most people assume that any phone problem is Southern Bell's, somewhere in the mass of broken wires. The problem may be inside your walls, caused by wet telephone jacks and wiring. If you are willing to spend an hour or so checking connections to potentially restore your service, keep reading.

There is little danger of shocking yourself. You may feel a tingling, but it will not hurt you. However, if you are unsure whether a wire is for your telephone, **DON'T TOUCH IT!**

HERE'S A LOOK AT THE EQUIPMENT IN YOUR HOUSE

Figure A

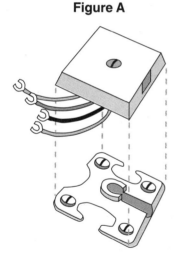

Figure B

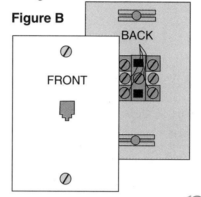

Figure C

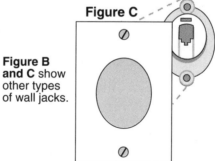

Figure B and C show other types of wall jacks.

Figure D

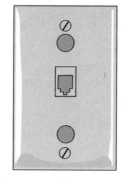

Figure A is the most common phone jack. The cover includes the modular jack and its wires. The base is mounted to the wall with telephone wiring connected to it.

Figure D has a metal (usually) cover on the jack and is for wall phones. All of these jacks have two common features: a modular phone jack and wires that connect the phone line to it.

Ron Weintraub

"People should get their plywood now. They should have the holes drilled now. If they measure and cut the plywood, they should be sure to treat the wood. Give it a coat of paint. If they cut it now and leave the boards in the garage, they will warp. If the boards are stored outside and they get wet they won't fit the window. Plywood should be stored flat, not on its side. Also, label each piece for the window it was cut for."

Shunequa Davis,
Age 17

"I'd stay, because of my 80-year-old great-grandmother. I know she wouldn't leave. Plus, you can't run from those things, you never know where they'll go. I think this time we'll buy more supplies and board up more. I'll also pay more attention to my pets."

MAKING CONNECTIONS

Figure G

The first place to go is to the phone connection outside your home. Bring a good phone with you. The phone connection, called a protector, is usually near the power meter or a water line. Don't touch the power meter. **Figure G** shows the most common phone connection for single-family homes. For most other dwellings see **Figure H**. Using a slot screwdriver,

unscrew the screw on the right side and open the cover. Inside are one or two modular phone jacks with a cord(s) plugged into them. Unplug the cord and wait 3 minutes for the phone line to reset (if it will). Plug the phone into each modular phone jack and check for a dial tone. If you get a dial tone, the problem is inside your home. If you don't, the trouble is outside and only Southern Bell can fix it.

WATER CAN SHORT OUT PHONE WIRING

There are several types of phone cables. They all have an outer covering that surrounds anywhere from three individual insulated wires up to 12 wires. Most houses wired within the last 30 years have one of two types of colored wire. The first has individual Red, Green, Yellow, and Black (**Figure E**). The phone line is generally on the Red and Green wires.

The second type has Blue/White, Orange/White, and Green/White pairs of

wires (**Figure F**). The pairs of wires are twisted and are made up of Blue with White and White with Blue, Orange with White and White with Orange, and Green with White and White with Green. The phone line is generally on the Blue/White pair.

When a jack gets wet the water shorts out the Red/Green or Blue/White wires and causes the entire line to go dead, even though all of the other jacks in your house may be fine. If you remove the short your phone will work again.

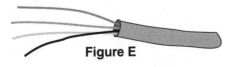

Figure E

Figure F

If you live in an apartment or condo, you probably have a jack in your kitchen that looks like **Figure H**. Unplug the small cord at the bottom of the jack, wait three minutes, and plug a good phone into the modular jack where the small cord was plugged in. If you have a dial tone the problem is inside your unit; if not, the trouble is outside and only Southern Bell can fix it.

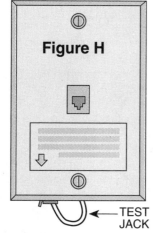

Figure H

← TEST JACK

A DIAL TONE

If you have a dial tone, you may want to fix the problem inside yourself. If you do, read on.

The leading cause of dead phone lines inside the home is wet modular jacks. Go to each phone jack in your house and unplug the phone cord. Look at the modular connection at the end of the cord and see if there is any discoloration or if it seems wet. If it does, leave the phone unplugged and move to the next jack. Repeat for every phone in the house, even ones that have no phones plugged into them.

USE WD-40

After you have checked all jacks, use WD-40 or a similar product and lightly spray each wet jack. This will force the water out and possibly restore the dial tone. Do the same thing to the modular connection on the end of your phone cords, gently wiping them dry.

CHECK FOR A DIAL TONE

Then, check your phones for a dial tone. If you have one, call someone and have them call you back. This will make sure the phone can ring.

CHECK EACH JACK OUTLET

If you do not have a dial tone, the problem is either with your in-house wiring or a jack that is still wet or damaged. Unscrew each jack outlet and check for water damage inside each outlet and the jack itself. Use an artist's paintbrush or a Q-Tip dipped in alcohol to gently wipe the modular jack and surrounding connections clean and dry. Repeat this procedure for each jack and try the phone line again.

MAY NEED PROFESSIONAL HELP

If you still have a problem, you will need professional help. Until help arrives, you can plug a cord into the outside conection and run it through a window to a phone.

REPORT PROBLEM, DIAL 611

If none of this works, the problem is probably outside and Southern Bell must fix it. You can report the problem by dialing 611 from a working phone. Follow up each report with a call once a week to make sure your problem hasn't been inadvertently shown as having been fixed. Above all, try to be patient. Remember: many other people will be having the same problems you are.

Raul Gonzalez

"I don't think we're going to get hit again — not like Andrew, anyway — maybe something smaller. We didn't put up shutters, nothing. I am just going to hold tight."

CHAPTER 7

Recovery

Picking up the pieces, cooking and cleaning are often simple–
just don't let fatigue get the best of you.

Water Precautions

After a hurricane, damaged water pipes can cause pressure to drop, possibly letting in contaminated ground water.

Here are some answers and tips for coping with water problems:

The feared problem with the water is bacterial contamination. The most common offenders: shigella and salmonella, which cause severe diarrhea. Untreated by antibiotics, these diseases can lead to life-threatening dehydration.

Disinfect any tap water you'll drink or use for cooking. Boil it for at least five minutes. Or use chemicals: eight drops of chlorine bleach (without scent or other additives) or tincture of iodine per gallon. Let the water sit at least 10 minutes before drinking.

Disinfect First

If cooking with tap water, disinfect it beforehand.

Water you saved in clean containers before the storm will probably be fine for two to three weeks. To be sure, add a couple of drops of chlorine or iodine per gallon before drinking.

For brushing teeth, use disinfected water.

Memories: Water damage to photos, keepsakes and other mementos may sometimes be repaired. Photos, for example, must be air-dried or frozen as soon as possible after the damage.

Pets shouldn't be given untreated tap water. They are as susceptible as people to diarrhea from impure water.

Wash dishes in tap water if you rinse them in extra-chlorinated water. Use about 15 drops of chlorine per quart of rinse water (or eight drops of iodine). This will leave a chlorine residue on the dishes to keep them clean until next use.

Showering or bathing in tap water is fine. If you cut yourself shaving, apply a disinfectant such as alcohol or antibiotic cream.

Contact Lenses

Contact lens wearers should use disinfected water to wash their hands before handling contacts.

People infected with HIV, the AIDS virus, are more susceptible than others to diseases carried by impure water. They should be especially careful about disinfecting drinking water.

People with water wells in areas of sewage contamination should avoid drinking the water. Well water can be disinfected, but high levels of chemicals such as nitrates will remain. These can be life-threatening to babies.

Keep soap and disinfected water near the toilet for washing hands. This is an important way to avoid spread of disease.

Use tap water or water from canals or ponds to flush toilets. As long as the tank is filled, a toilet always can be flushed.

If flushing the toilet isn't possible and

If You Get Sick

If diarrhea strikes, drink plenty of fluids to avoid dehydration. High-sugar fluids, such as Gatorade, apple juice or soft drinks, will make it worse. But these drinks can be used if diluted with an equal amount of water.

Children especially are at risk of dehydration when diarrhea strikes. Danger signs: decreased urination, sunken eyes, extreme thirst, unusual drowsiness and no tears when the child cries.

For adults, there's a way to ward off diarrheal disease if it hits a family: Take two tablets of Pepto-Bismol (bismuth salicylate) every half-hour for a total of eight doses. This is not recommended for anyone under 16.

emergency authorities haven't set up portable toilets in your area, dig a pit toilet. Cover the waste daily with dirt sprinkled with bleach.

Food Safety Rules To Memorize

Fresh milk spoils rapidly without refrigeration. Custards and creamed foods also are dangerous as are cream cheese, cheese spread and cottage cheese.

Hamburger, pork, fish and poultry spoil rapidly without refrigeration and should be discarded if they've been without cooling for several hours. Don't trust your sense of smell.

DON'T: Make a bunch of hard-boiled eggs and plan to store them at room temperature, eating them over a few days. It's a recipe for food poisoning.

DO: Clean out the refrigerator if the power has been off for more than two days. Throw away perishables. Wipe the interior with baking soda and water.

Without air conditioning, food waste will start to smell rapidly. Use small plastic garbage bags, big enough for one meal's refuse. Tie or seal and place in a larger bag or can outdoors.

If the power's off for one or two days only and your freezer is full of big cuts of meat or casseroles and you keep your door shut, your food probably will stay frozen and be fine.

A full freezer stays cold longer than a less-full one. (Consider filling plastic jugs of water to fill it.)

Meats and solid items stay frozen longer than baked goods.

Refreezing partially thawed food is risky. Generally, if the foods still contain ice crystals, they're OK to refreeze, though their quality may suffer.

Dry ice keeps food frozen for about one to four days.

Cooking Without A Stove

Without power, cooking becomes a survival skill.

Here are some tips to make it more appetizing. Fresh goods you can keep without refrigeration. Palatable combinations of canned foods to turn out salads, stews, soups and main dishes.

No perishable commodities, such as milk or butter, are included. What is assumed is some kind of heat source for cooking — camp stove, hot plate or electric skillet run off a generator, gas or charcoal grill or a plain old campfire. Cooking times are kept to a minimum — heating foods through, basically.

Extension Service Advice

Canned goods are the best bet for those without refrigeration and with limited ability to cook. Choose a wide range — canned meats, seafoods, fruits, vegetables.

Try to avoid leftovers. Aim for only as much food as your family will eat in one meal; if you have a choice, use small cans. If food is left over, eat it by the next meal or throw it out.

A variety of salad dressings and seasonings can help ward off monotony. So can a variety of breads — pita, whole wheat, rye.

Some fresh goods last well outside of the refrigerator — onions, carrots, cucumbers, tomatoes, apples, pears, plums. Even lettuce (but keep it out of direct sunlight).

Chocolate drink mixes can make powdered or shelf-stable milk more palatable. Dehydrated onions, dehydrated bell peppers and spice mixes such as cajun seasoning improve the taste of canned foods.

When shopping for canned goods, consider canned corned beef, tuna, chunk chicken, turkey and fish. Canned seafood such as shrimp or clams can be added to soups or mix with chopped onion, oil and lemon to make a sandwich spread.

Also look at products you might avoid in better times — canned potatoes, boxed scalloped potato mixes, canned tomato wedges, canned mushrooms, bottled spaghetti sauces.

Garlic keeps very well outside the refrigerator and adds a jolt of flavor to anything. The same is true of lemons and limes.

Canned zucchini in tomato sauce is really good. So are canned stewed tomatoes. Canned green chilies and bottled salsa add a big dose of flavor.

Cooking Tips

Instant rice needs only boiling (or very hot) water to reconstitute it.

Cast iron is good for makeshift cooking on a camp stove or grill because it retains heat well and is virtually indestructible. Its handle gets very hot, so be careful. Disposable aluminum pie pans are also good for this kind of cooking. Otherwise, use old pots and pans over charcoal because they'll become blackened on the outside. Obviously, though, you'll use what you have.

If you have access to a generator, hook up an electric skillet with a cover. It uses much less power than a range.

If you have a charcoal or gas grill and an outdoor area to use them, your cooking options expand greatly. You can cook just about anything in a foil packet; use heavy-duty wrap and make one large package of, say, vegetables, or individual servings. Sprinkle with salt and pepper, drizzle with oil and dried herbs or other seasonings and seal. You can roast regular or sweet pota-

toes on the grill, too.

To cook large pieces of meat or a whole chicken, use the "indirect" method. This means building a charcoal fire on the sides of the grate instead of in the middle. (You can do this with a gas grill, too; check the manual or just follow the same principles.) When the coals have burned down, set a foil drip pan in the center (where the coals aren't) and set the chicken or roast on the rack over the pan. Then cover the grill and cook.

Use As Oven

The grill will act like an oven and roast your dinner. Timing will depend on the size of what you're cooking; don't keep lifting the lid to peek, but wait about an hour to test with a meat thermometer. Poultry needs to reach 170 degrees in the thigh, 180 in the breast, to be safe. Pork is done at 160 degrees. Rare beef will read 140 degrees; medium is about 160. If you don't have a meat thermometer, test by pricking with a fork or cutting with a knife to have a look. Poultry juices will run clear.

You can also use a grill to heat canned foods in a saucepan or disposable foil pan, but be careful. Wait until the flames have died down and then watch closely; this is easier on a gas grill that you can regulate. You may heat food in opened cans on a grill; don't do this with unopened cans, which can explode.

Try These Ideas

Add a little vinegar or a squeeze of lemon or lime juice, if you have it, to stews or salads just before serving for some tang and freshness. A little vinegar plus any canned fruit can make a sweet-and-sour sauce for meats.

Use evaporated milk when you would

Julian Fernandez,
Age 9

"One day I was playing with my friend Mark Sebastian. I turned on the TV. The news was on. The news said there was a hurricane coming that was called Hurricane Andrew. One day later the news said that the hurricane was definitely coming. When the hurricane came, I went to my grandmother's home. I was there when the hurricane hit. When I went back to my house, I found that a big fat branch had crashed into my room window. I started to cry when I went into my house. I thought that I would not live at my house again but then I thought that maybe we could fix it. That's what we did. Now I'm living in my house again because there's always hope."

CLEANUP TIPS

You want to clean up the mess the storm has left. But before you get started, remember:

Couch potatoes will need weeks and not days to move all the debris.

Drink plenty of fluids. Sun and work are a killer.

Wear sunscreen and a hat.

Wear work boots. They're hot, but they'll protect you from nails, glass, wire and critters.

Put on light-colored clothing, including pants, for protection.

Wear work gloves.

Lift with the legs, not with the back.

If you can't identify something, don't touch it. Be especially wary of downed electrical wires.

Don't use a chain saw for the first time to clear your yard. Wear goggles.

Don't burn trash.

Ask for help when you need it. Rest when the load gets too heavy.

ordinarily use cream.

Some pepperoni is stored at room temperature routinely. Chop it up and add to bean salads or stir into bottled spaghetti sauce with a can of mushrooms to serve over noodles.

Stir some bottled teriyaki sauce and spicy mustard into baked beans.

Doctor baked beans with A-1 sauce, maple syrup, catsup and Worcestershire sauce.

Heat canned black-eyed peas with some chopped onion and green pepper, then serve over instant rice.

A Fast Chowder

Make a fast tuna chowder with a can of potatoes, a can or two of tuna, a bottle of clam juice, a chopped onion, a chopped carrot and a can of white beans. For red chowder, add canned tomatoes. For white, add powdered or evaporated milk.

Mix catsup, vegetable oil, vinegar, sugar and garlic for a salad dressing.

Jazz up canned beef stew with fresh carrots and onions and a can of mushrooms, and warm through in a deep skillet.

Make an easy peanut sauce for noodles by mixing one half cup each hot water and peanut butter, 2 teaspoons soy sauce, 2 teaspoons vinegar, 2 teaspoons sesame oil (optional), 2 minced garlic cloves and a teaspoon of sugar. If you have any green onions or cucumbers, chop them up and add to cooked noodles with the dressing

Tuna Casserole

Mix instant rice with a can of peas, a can of tuna, chopped onion, celery, garlic and a can of cream soup, then heat for a stove-top tuna casserole.

Stir canned white beans or chick peas into bottled spaghetti sauce for a boost of protein.

Make a quick soup with onions, car-

rots, canned tomatoes, canned potatoes and canned broth. Stir in some canned turkey and broth, water or wine.

Mix a can of white beans with a can of Italian-style stewed tomatoes, some garlic and thyme, then serve with rice or noodles if you have them.

Turn boxed scalloped potato mix into soup by adding chicken broth and evaporated milk.

Makeshift Kitchen And Other Power Substitutes

Living without electricity requires some inventiveness. Consider these suggestions for the kitchen, lights at night and appliances.

Field Kitchen

A garage, carport or roofed patio would be an ideal spot for a temporary kitchen. This is what you'll need:

A surface to prepare food. This could be a card table or any folding table. A door or sheet of plywood on sawhorses also will serve.

A large cooler and bags of ice to keep food fresh. Buy only the amount of fresh food your family can consume in one meal. Rely on canned foods for safety's sake.

A charcoal or propane gas grill or a camp stove. Do not bring these grills inside. They are called outdoor grills for a reason: You could set your house on fire. They also use up oxygen, and it's hot enough inside already.

Any cabinets that can be salvaged from your damaged kitchen can be used to store canned goods, sodas, paper towels and plates. If they can't be salvaged, sturdy cardboard boxes will do.

Lights

For lighting at night, many people opt for fuel-based lanterns. Use them indoors only sparingly because they eat up oxygen. Some people try to get around the power loss with portable generators. Follow instructions carefully. Generators installed incorrectly can backfeed and injure workers trying to restore power.

Appliance Safety

Unplug all appliances so that when the power finally comes back on, they won't be harmed by surges or turn off all circuit breakers.

Bill Clinton,
U.S. president,
after Andrew

"Amidst the wreckage, there is hope. Community leaders and residents are unified in their commitment to rebuild. Individuals whose own homes and lives were destroyed in the disaster work tirelessly to restore the larger community. They and I see the hurricane as the turning point that will spark a rebuilt community of quality housing, functioning neighborhoods, thriving tourism, agriculture and jobs. The federal government can and must help South Dade recover. We are providing funding and delivering the leadership and coordination which will help bring the South Dade effort together."

Survival Cooking: Healthy eating is possible without the usual appliances. Canned goods are the best bet. But some fresh goods last well outside the refrigerator such as onions, carrots, cucumbers, apples, pears and plums.

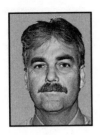

Scott Berger

"After the shock of a hurricane, a tree should only be trimmed to remove broken and damaged branches. Cover root balls with wet blankets. The tree can survive this way for months before replanting is required. If a tree has green underneath its bark, it is still alive."

Saving Appliances

Here are some things you can do to minimize damage and salvage household goods after a storm:

If your stove, washer, dryer, microwave or other appliance got wet, be extremely cautious. All appliances, including radios, TV sets and room air conditioners should not be used until they have been inspected and re-conditioned where necessary by a qualified service technician, using manufacturer's advice. Dangers include electrical shock, leaking gas or food contamination if the equipment is used before it's safe.

Area rugs should be taken outdoors to dry. It's best to keep them out of direct sunlight. If possible, dry them on a covered patio or porch. Take water-stained rugs to a rug cleaner as soon as possible.

For sodden wall-to-wall carpet, lift it and remove the wet padding. If you have electricity, you can rent a special vacuum that will extract the water from the carpet.

To keep chair and table legs from staining wet carpet, wrap aluminum foil around the feet. If possible, elevate upholstered sofas with wood blocks or Styrofoam so the carpet will dry evenly under it.

Hang To Dry

Hang wet clothing outdoors to dry, but not in direct sunlight. If you have power, wash and dry as soon as possible, according to care labels.

Wet draperies should be taken down as soon as possible and spread out to dry. After they dry, take them to the dry cleaners. Some water stains won't come out. If you are without electricity, dry draperies outdoors until you can launder according to care labels.

If your home got water inside, get your wood furniture out of the wet but don't put it outdoors. The sun would do even more damage. The furniture may need to be cleaned, treated and sealed.

Wet upholstered furniture should be elevated if it's resting on carpet. If you have a covered patio, move sofas and chairs outdoors to dry. Do not place them in direct sunlight. You may need a machine to extract the water.

Upholstery that is thoroughly soaked may not be salvageable. It might be re-upholstered if the frame is sturdy.

If you have electricity, wash blankets and comforters according to the care label. Wool blankets and some comforters may need dry cleaning. Hang them out to dry in the meantime.

Dry pillows outdoors, but not in direct sunlight. If you have power, put wet pillows in the clothes dryer. Some say a clean tennis shoe tossed in the dryer with a pillow will fluff it up.

Broom, Bleach, Shovel

Cleaning up kitchens and bathrooms after a storm is a daunting task.

Where do you begin? The kitchen first, then the baths.

Here's how to go about it:

The Kitchen

Make a list of supplies. If there is thick mud on the floor, get a shovel and a container to put it in. You will need bleach, disinfectant, clean rags, gardening gloves to pick up broken glass and rubber gloves for scrubbing. Also: a broom, brush and dust pan. If you don't have a dust pan, use a newspaper folded like one.

Clean up mud and debris on the floor first. If you're shoveling, place the container — a sturdy cardboard box will do — next to the area you are working on. Fill the container, then dump it outside.

Once you get the bulk of the mud out, throw out broken and cracked dishes and chipped glasses.

Clean Top To Bottom

Clean from top to bottom so you won't drip dirty water on clean surfaces. Add a few drops of bleach to the cleaning water in case the water has bacteria in it. Clean all of one type of surface first. Clean the ceiling first, followed by the walls, cabinets, then counter tops. Then clean inside the cabinets.

To clean appliances, use a good grease cutter such as Formula 409.

For the inside of refrigerators and freezers (which should be unplugged), a baking soda solution is ideal. Wipe it on, then wash it off with clean water. If the refrigerator gasket has mildew, use a mild bleach solution to kill it. Wipe off coils on the back of the refrigerator.

When the refrigerator defrosted, it probably leaked into the drain pan at the back of the appliance. Take off the safe plate at the bottom, pull the drain pan out, empty it outdoors, wash and dry it in the sun. Ventilate the refrigerator/ freezer with both doors open.

Once the refrigerator is sanitized, place an open box of baking soda or activated charcoal inside to absorb odors. If odors persist in the house because of the refrigerator, set bowls of white vinegar around to absorb the smell.

If the dishwasher smells funny, sprinkle baking soda on the bottom and keep the door open. If you've stored dishes in the machine, wash them by hand.

Bleach is a good sanitizer and deodorizer, but you also need a good disinfectant to kill bacteria.

Baths

Bathtubs that have been storing water should be sanitized before they are used for bathing.

Toilets also should be sanitized, as brackish or contaminated water may have come up the pipes.

Wash the tub and toilet with bleach.

It's also a good idea to wash the whole bathroom with water containing bleach or ammonia. Any Lysol-type disinfectant also can be used.

Wear rubber gloves while you are doing this disinfecting to protect your skin from irritation.

HERE'S A TIP

If you are unable to tackle a huge cleaning project as a result of the hurricane, most homeowner insurance policies will cover the cost of professional cleaning.

Take before photographs of the kitchen, bath and other areas of the home to be cleaned as proof of their condition.

Use services that are licensed, bonded and insured.

WHAT YOU'LL NEED

Before you start cleaning, assemble these supplies:

Plenty of plastic trash bags, paper towels, clean rags.

A shovel for mud.

Boxes or other containers to remove mud and debris.

Broom and dust pan.

Bleach, disinfectant, clean water.

Buckets, mops, scrub brushes.

Gardening gloves to pick up broken glass; rubber gloves for scrubbing.

Juan Travieso

"If a hurricane comes again, I will just work real hard every day to help people rebuild. I will work every day except Sunday. I love this country."

Roof Repairs

While waiting for licensed contractors, there are two temporary remedies for leaks you can use.

But before climbing atop your home, know this: Licensed, insured contractors hesitated to offer this advice because roof work is dangerous. It is easy to slip, particularly on wet tile; and there is danger from tree branches, power lines and ladders.

Repairs are made from the outside. On the inside, set up buckets under the leaky areas and punch a pencil or screwdriver into the lowest part of the ceiling around the leaks to relieve the water pressure.

On the outside of the roof, you can use plastic sheeting or tar paper. The smallest holes may be patched by using a trowel to spread roofing plastic cement over them.

Plastic sheeting: This is the most temporary measure. Take heavy plastic sheets — a brand name is Visqueen — and use roofing nails to fasten them around the hole.

If you can find 2-by-4s, square off the hole with the wood first. Then wrap the plastic around the wood, and nail down the wood, said Jeff Manson of Manson Restoration Services in Boynton Beach.

If you can't get wood or nails, use bricks, cement blocks or sandbags to hold down the plastic.

Roofing paper: This is known as tar paper or roofing felt. Find it in the building-materials sections of stores. It is applied with trowel-grade roofing plastic cement and a trowel.

The paper generally is sold in rolls by weight — 15-, 30- and 90-weight paper are common — per 100 square feet.

The paper is best applied in overlapping layers — alternating the cement and paper — from the bottom of the roof upward.

Contractor Tips

The National Roofing Contractors Association can help you find reputable roofing contractors. Send a self-addressed, stamped envelope (two first class stamps) to the NRCA, Buying a New Roof, 10255 W. Higgins Rd., Suite 600, Rosemont, Ill. 60018.

The group offers these tips:

■ Check for a permanent place of business, telephone number, tax identification number and occupational license. A professional will have these readily available.

■ Choose a company with a good track record.

■ Ask the contractor for proof of insurance. Insist on seeing copies of both liability coverage and workers' compensation certificates.

■ Find out if the contractor is bonded and licensed.

■ Be sure the contractor can provide a manufacturer's warranty. Beware of unrealistic, long-term warranties.

■ Ask for a list of references and completed projects. Check with past customers to see if they were satisfied with the materials and workmanship.

■ Call the Department of Professional Regulation to check for complaints against a contractor. DPR's number is (800) 342-7940.

■ Insist on a written proposal, and examine it carefully.

Spotting Roof Problems

Resist the urge to get up on a ladder to take a closer look at your damaged roof. Leave that to a professional. Here's some inspection advice.

From The Ground

If you have a two-story home, use binoculars.

Look for torn or missing shingles and problems in the valleys — where two sloping sections join at an angle. Because water flows heavily in the valleys, they are especially vulnerable.

A Closer Look

If you must see for yourself, wear non-slip, rubber-soled shoes and use a firmly braced or tied-off ladder equipped with rubber safety feet.

Don't Walk On The Roof

You could dislodge the protective surface granules, diminishing waterproofing effectiveness. You also could fall off or through a weak, damaged roof.

If you find large accumulations of shingle surface granules in the gutters, it doesn't necessarily mean the roof needs to be replaced. But the roof should be inspected by a contractor.

For a tile roof, check for cracked, missing or loose pieces of roofing material. For asphalt or wood-shingle roofs, look for protruding nails.

On flat roofs, look for bare spots in the gravel surface and check for standing water.

Take a close look at the flashing on chimneys, vents, skylights, wall/ roof junctions and other areas.

Check television antennas and other add-ons — leaks can result from improper sealing of openings made in the roof.

Laura Bradley,
Age 11

"Grab a stuffed animal to hold on to because it will help you relax. Stay close to your family and try to cover your head in case something comes through the ceiling."

Nailing Down: Temporary roof repairs can be made with heavy plastic sheets and roofing nails. Wear rubber-soled shoes when working on the roof.

Doreen Barton

"We put a small kiddie pool for cooling off in the back yard."

Keeping Your Cool

Face it, rivulets of sweat and great globs of grime from head to toe are just not cool. But, then, neither is your house without electricity and related pleasures like air conditioning and hot showers.

But there are some things you can do to stay cool and clean.

First, the standard ones: Drink plenty of fluids. Try to get in the breeze and in the shade. Wear lightweight clothing, preferably all cotton, linen or silk. Endure cold showers.

A Few Other Ideas

The first: Pitch the mattresses. Sleep in a hammock, so your whole body is exposed to air on all sides.

Second, think green. And blue, and white. Green and blue — the colors of water and the forest — have been reported to make people feel cooler. White absorbs less heat from the sun than other colors.

Also, cotton sheets with a high thread count are cool to the touch. And try draping a wet washcloth over your feet at night.

If you're out in the sun, wrap wet handkerchiefs around your forehead and neck.

There are some scientific reasons why applying water or wet cloths helps you keep cool. There's less body fat in the head and neck, as well as around the wrists and ankles. Body fat acts as insulation, keeping heat in. Wet cloths applied to areas with little body fat will cool the body more quickly.

There are a couple of things you can do around the house to keep heat out. Cover windows from the inside with blinds or drapes to keep the room cool. Tape aluminum foil, shiny side out, on the inside of west- or east-facing windows. This prevents a greenhouse effect caused by heat bouncing from the glass to the blinds or drapes and back again.

If you want a hot bath try a sun or solar shower — the shower-in-a-bag well-known to boaters and campers. You can rig it up in your back yard.

Here's How It Works

Fill the plastic bag with water and hang it outside in the sun. The bag comes with a shower nozzle. When the water is warm, douse yourself with it — bathing suit optional.

Stores that carry camping and boating equipment are likely to have these showers.

Light and Airy: Hammocks are cooler for sleeping than mattresses because they allow air to circulate around the body.

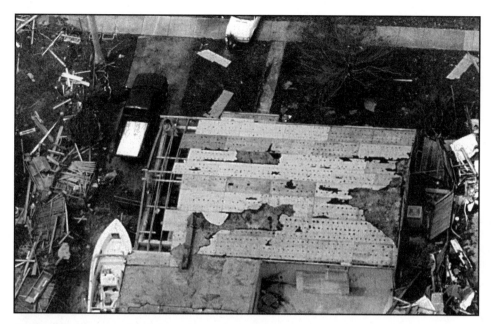

Dirty Pool: Remove debris from the pool. Superchlorinate the water until electricity is restored or help arrives. Keep swimmers out of the water while it's superchlorinated.

Reviving Your Pool

Without electricity to filter and vacuum pools, that shimmering lagoon in your back yard can turn into a fetid mosquito haven.

To maintain reasonable water quality while you wait for the power to be restored or for pool maintenance personnel to fix damage to pumps or filtration systems, follow these steps:

Remove all debris from the pool.

If there's dirt on the pool bottom, a $30 device called a Leafmaster might help. The Leafmaster, which attaches to a pool brush handle, uses a garden hose to blast dirt or sediment from the bottom into a collection bag. It probably won't be much help if there's lots of mud, sand or sludge in the pool.

Add a chlorinator, either in the form of the 10 percent sodium hypochlorite solution sold in the familiar yellow jugs or the 65 percent calcium hypochlorite granules commonly known as shock.

Superchlorinate the pool according to the manufacturer's instructions. Doing so will restore the water's familiar color, but the pool will appear cloudy.

Maintain the water in its superchlorinated state until electricity is restored or help arrives.

Don't allow anyone in the water while it's superchlorinated. The generally safe level of chlorination for swimming is 1.0 to 3.0 parts per million.

Chris Fulmer

"Have plenty of food and games for the kids to keep them busy on the morning after while the adults clean up. Wet wipes, Gatorade and anti-diarrhea medication are all important during the aftermath. We would have made more contact with our neighbors before the storm so that they would have known where to seek safe haven if their house blew away — two nearby families fled in their cars during the eye and were very frightened and slightly injured. We set up a phone chain in order to let out-of-town family members know we were OK even if we could get only one phone call out. We sent a form letter to everyone in our address book as soon as possible to let them know how we were."

Eddie Persons

"I wasn't affected by the hurricane directly, but I did go down to help the victims. We brought food and water, lots of water. We brought personal hygiene products, baby food and clothes.

It's important for everyone to pitch in and help our neighbors after something like this happens."

Pool Repairs

If your pool has gouges in the Marcite interior coating or other structural damage, you'll need an expert to help. Choose one carefully.

The state issues three types of licenses for swimming pool contractors: commercial, residential and pool servicing. Some counties also have licensing requirements.

To find out if the contractor you are considering is licensed, call the licensing board's records office at (904) 359-6310.

Get estimates from several contractors and ask contractors to provide names and numbers of clients they've recently done work for so you can see if those owners are satisfied with the work.

Wet Electronic Gear

If a storm gives your TV set or stereo system a bath, don't throw it out right away. It may be salvageable.

First, of course, you need the power restored. Then you need to follow a couple of safety rules:

Before you try these procedures, make sure both the equipment and the area around it — cabinets, floor, etc. — are completely dry to avoid the danger of electric shock.

Don't Be Shocked

If you have an outside antenna, make sure it is not touching a power line before you touch the connections on the back of your TV set.

Never open a TV set to attempt to dry it inside by yourself. Most picture tubes maintain a dangerously high voltage of about 25,000 volts and stay charged even when the set is unplugged.

Ready? Here's some advice:

Unplug the set and let it dry for as long as possible; once moisture on the outside has evaporated, plug it in.

If the set comes on, keep it on for no more than 10 minutes. Then turn it off and let it sit for another 20 to 30 minutes. Repeat the procedure, letting the set run for 20 minutes this time. This gives components inside the heat needed to dry off.

Warning: If you leave the TV on for normal viewing without using this procedure, moisture inside the set could burn out some of its inner components.

If your TV did not get wet but has been off for four or more days, follow the same procedure. Without air conditioning, moisture from the atmosphere may have seeped inside.

If the set does not come on when you switch it on, it's best to take it to a service shop. In many cases, repairs may be minor, so don't throw your set out — it could cost more to replace it.

Dry Your VCR

Videocassette recorders require the same drying-out procedure as TV sets, except they are somewhat safer: There is no tube that maintains a dangerous voltage.

First, plug the VCR in and see if the indicators on the front panel light up. If they do, you've got power, and you can proceed to a test.

Unlike TV sets, most VCRs have a dew sensor that detects internal moisture. If it does, the VCR will not play a tape. Don't worry if your machine doesn't seem to work at first; just leave it plugged in and use the above procedure, alternately turning the machine on and off. Eventually it should dry itself out.

If the front panel's clock and lights do not go on, it's time to see a technician. Again, it's usually worth investigating repairs before tossing it out.

Other electronic equipment, such as stereo systems, portable radio-stereos, laser-disc players and the like can be tested using the same procedure as for VCRs.

Jeff Lefcourt

"It would be a real good idea to buy a chain saw. We didn't own one right after Andrew and when it came time to rent one, you couldn't."

There's Hope: Unplug TV and let it dry for as long as possible; it may be salvageable. Before checking damaged electronic gear, make sure both the equipment and area around it are thoroughly dry to avoid the danger of electric shock.

Danielle Hirsch,
Age 9

"We also might even have to move and will always remember this horrible time. My family is a great one so we'll try to forget it. We will still all love each other so we will be all right. We will also still be together — that's the most important thing of all. I will always be sad, but in a way I would be kind of happy, but the main thing is, as I said, we are together."

Art Repair

Got a clammy Cezanne print or a cracked ceramic bowl? Regardless of the type of art, the prevention of mold or mildew and stabilization of structural damage is key, restorers and conservators say.

Following are examples of treatment for different types of art. The list is not intended to be comprehensive.

Mold damage. It can be prevented by providing air flow (even if it means only opening windows), leaving lights on, lowering the humidity below 70 percent (dehumidifiers are recommended), removing wet liners and blotting excess moisture from the back with paper towels. Do not try to rub off mold. Here's how this gets tricky.

Some items can be washed, some can't; some should be covered, some not; for some you can use absorbent material on the face, some only on the back.

Photographs, for instance, must be air-dried or frozen as soon as possible after the damage. If they are air-dried, they must be unframed and separated, allowed to drain excess water, and spread out to dry face up on paper towels or blotters or clean cloths.

If they are stuck to the glass, frame or each other, freeze them in plastic bags, with wax paper or other nonwoven polyester material separating them.

But for a painting, the advice is: remove it from the wall, remove any backing board from the painting, absorb moisture from canvas reverse by dabbing paper towels or other absorbent material and lean the painting against a table or chair to allow free air flow around it.

Stabilization. With broken ceramics, glass, stone, metals or organics (basketry, leather, wood, bone and ivory), the fragments should be individually wrapped in tissue paper. This keeps them from rubbing together.

Put all wrapped pieces flat on the bottom of a box. Large pieces should be padded with paper or bubble packing.

Water-Weary Piano

Pianos may seem like a picayune problem in a storm's aftermath, but if one endured the fury with you, it needs some loving care. Even if water merely danced around it, a free damage appraisal is worth asking for.

An appraisal will determine if the piano can be salvaged. Get a quotation in writing for the cost of repair, rebuilding, refinishing or replacement. Restoring a piano can cost $2,000 to $4,000.

The longer the damage is untreated the worse it becomes. Turning the air conditioning on high is bad for a piano. Start low and gradually increase the coolness.

Get an appraisal for repair or replacement before sending the piano out. Some insurance adjusters want to see the piano first.

Pianos are made of wood and swell when they get wet. The finishes are harmed, the strings rust and the damage in general might be so bad that repairs could rival the cost of a new piano.

Call professionals to remove large, uprooted trees or heavy, precarious limbs. You may want to proceed with less dangerous work yourself.

FOLLOW THESE SAFETY TIPS

■ Make certain that area is free of **power lines**.

■ Use proper **safety equipment**: heavy gloves, safety goggles, heavy boots, long-sleeve shirt, long pants. Tie long hair back or wear a hat.

■ If using a **ladder**, follow safety instructions printed on the ladder. Don't take chances.

■ If using a **chain saw**,

– Wear a **hardhat** and **earplugs**.
– Remove any **brush or limbs** that may catch the tip of the saw and cause it to buck back at you.
– When **starting the chain saw**, place it on the ground with your right foot through the rear handle and your left

hand on the front handle. Before pulling starter cord, make sure the saw is at least 10 feet from the fuel.
– **When cutting heavy limbs**, make sure you know which way they will fall. Have in mind a path for retreat.

– Keep your **head and body** out of line with the blade. It could kick back and injure you.
– **Never** raise the saw above your head and chest.
– **Never** walk around with the saw running.

CHAIN SAW CUTTING

Cutting through wood with a chain saw is accomplished by slowly pivoting the blade at the base, moving the tip up and down.

1, 3

2, 4

1. Start the cut at the base of the blade.
2. Pivot the tip of the blade downward.
3. Lower the back of the saw.
4. Lower the tip again.
5. Continue rocking motion until cut is complete.

TRIMMING HEAVY BRANCHES

Second cut First cut Final cut

A rope may be needed to support the weight of the branch after it is cut. Make the first cut halfway through the underside of the branch, 18" from the tree trunk. Make a second cut on the top and farther out on the limb. The weight of the limb will cause it to break off. Trim the remaining 18" nearly flush with trunk.

REPLANTING SMALL TREES

You might be able to save small trees and palms that have toppled by simply pushing them back up and replanting them. Do it soon, though, before the roots dry out. Also, trim back tree limbs and lower palm fronds to reduce water demands on the roots.

SELECTING A NEW LEADER FOR A "TOPPED" TREE

Trees with a strong central shoot grow as cylinders or pyramids. If the top is damaged, restore the leader by cutting back to the nearest healthy side shoot. Lash a bamboo cane to the trunk so that it projects two feet above the top. Bend and lash the new leader to the cane. Allow it to straighten out for two years. Make sure the lashing doesn't constrict the growth of the tree.

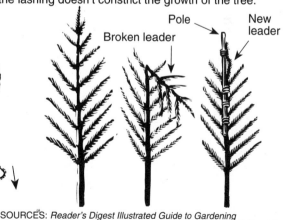

Pole New leader Broken leader

SOURCES: *Reader's Digest Illustrated Guide to Gardening*
Ortho books: *Guide to Garden Equipment* and *All About Pruning*

CHAPTER 8

Repair and Rebuild

Down is definitely not out. Adjusters, contractors, stores will help you put your life back together.

Finding The Damage

Rebuilding your damaged home may mean tearing into it even more than a hurricane did.

The builder may have to rip down ceilings to get at roof trusses, or tear out walls to assess water damage or electrical corrosion.

It can be more difficult, time-consuming and costly than building from scratch — and the process is compounded by raw emotions that grind like so many pieces of glass into dealings with contractors.

Here, then, is a sampling of what to expect.

Thoroughly assess the damage. Go over the entire house. Reputable contractors won't rebuild one portion correctly but leave defective work in the undamaged part of the house.

Among the toughest aspects of assessment is finding hidden damage. And, to homeowners already reeling from the destruction, it may mean damaging even more of their home — in order to repair it.

To get to the roof trusses, for instance, the contractor may have to tear out ceilings and soffits.

The strong winds may have moved the trusses, which loosened the plates that

Top Priority: You can fix some problems temporarily, but hire a contractor for major repairs. Strong winds may have weakened the structural integrity of a roof, and the damage may not be readily apparent.

hold joints together that are engineered to carry the load of the roof. All that weakens the structural integrity of the roof — something that is not easily seen.

Or the wind may have lifted the roof and set it right back down again. As a result, there could be little cracks where the wall meets the soffit. An engineer will be able to tell if the cracking is excessive.

Here's another concern: Walls seemingly undamaged may actually be holding water.

If a wall is within a 5-foot radius of a water stain on your ceiling, chances are that water probably has gone into the wall.

You may not notice the damage until weeks or months later. You'll have to take everything out from inside the house down to the masonry.

Or, try this one: Your home is older and was built according to an earlier code requirement. Fixing the damaged portion in accord with an updated code may require bringing the entire house up to the new code requirements.

As a result of the myriad considerations of an assessment, contractors generally ask that you get a structural engineer's report, too.

Contractors say that to rebuild, you've got to tear down. Just how much is the tricky part, and it usually already has been determined during the assessment.

Demolition also can tack an extra 10 percent or so onto the rebuilding cost.

Once you understand that rebuilding

Sarah Graber,
Age 9

"Our neighbors asked us if we wanted to stay at their house. Lisa Soldana, the neighbor, offered me ice cream before we lost the power. During the hurricane we were all in one room with five cats and two dogs. That was exciting. The roof got cracks in it so the floor got wet. We had to wear shoes to bed. The next day, it was so windy that when I walked out the first time, I fell. My dad took me, my sister Alexis and my brother Jack to our house to see what it looked like. When we got there, a lot of people were crying. When I looked at my house, I began to cry. The next day everybody was working. They all looked tired, hot and sweaty. When dinner time came, the Schardts [George and Jean] asked some people if they wanted to come to their house for dinner. Every night we ate dinner together under the stars with all our wonderful neighbors."

often means working in reverse to how the home was first constructed, you'll begin to understand why it can take 30 percent longer than building from scratch.

The rebuilding contractor often works from the outside inward — instead of inside out.

Contractors vary on how much more rebuilding costs than new construction — from 10 percent to 50 percent.

Glass Often Not Enough To Ward Off Damage

Wind alone is not going to make glass break. A wind-driven object can make it break. Whether it will break, or how it breaks, depends on the type of glass, the object hitting it and the speed and angle at which the object hits.

The most common types of glass sold in South Florida are annealed, tempered, laminated and Thermopane.

Common, ordinary, everyday glass is annealed glass. Treat it with heat, and it becomes tempered glass. Sandwich two panes around a plastic or fiber inner layer, and that's laminated glass.

An auto windshield is an example of laminated glass. When hit, one or both panes of glass may shatter, but the inner layer tends to hold the bits of glass in place. This could limit interior damage.

According to Monsanto, a manufacturer of laminated glass, replacing annealed glass with laminated glass would cost 15 percent to 25 percent more per window.

Seal a layer of air or gas between two panes of glass and Thermopane glass is the result.

In general, the strength of glass will decline by roughly 20 percent in the first year. When glass is about 5 years old, the basic strength has been reduced by about

half. Still, wind alone won't cause it to fail.

Will anything protect a window from flying debris?

Shutters can be engineered to stop what breaks the glass, but they have limits.

For example, if a section of your neighbor's roof slams into your hurricane shutters, chances are good that the window will break, no matter what type of glass is used.

Starting Point: Thorough assessment shows obvious and hidden damage. Rebuilding often entails some demolition, and the whole process can take 30 percent longer than building from scratch.

Furniture To Save

What to save? What to throw away? These are questions thousands of storm victims ask as they sort through their damaged homes.

Here's some advice on salvaging and repairing furniture.

First, decide which pieces are worth restoring based on extent of damage, cost of the article, sentimental value and cost of restoration.

Antiques are probably worth the time, effort and expense. If damage appears minor, you might be able to clean, re-glue and refinish antiques at home. Extensive repair or re-veneering should be done at a reliable repair shop.

Solid wood furniture usually can be restored, unless damage is severe. You probably will need to clean, dry and re-glue it. Slightly warped boards may be removed and straightened.

Wood veneered furniture is usually not worth the cost and effort of repair, unless it has great monetary or sentimental value. If veneer is loose in just a few places, you may be able to repair it.

Conserving Cushions

Upholstered furniture may be salvageable. Clean and dry flooded pieces; remove mildew. If damage is extensive, you may have to replace padding and upholstery. Since this is expensive, it might be wiser to just buy new furniture.

Any furniture worth repairing should be cleaned, dried and stored in a dry, warm, well-ventilated place until you can get to it.

Upholstered furniture that has been submerged may be too far gone. But if the piece is worth saving:

Remove furniture coverings using a ripping tool, hammer or tack puller, screwdriver or chisel.

Remove all tacks from the frame.

Wash coverings, if they are cotton. Other fabrics will have to be dry cleaned.

Throw away all cotton stuffing. You can dry, fumigate and reuse padding made of materials other than cotton.

Wipe off springs and frame. Dry all metal parts and paint them with rust-inhibiting paint. Oil the springs.

Store wood furniture where it will dry slowly.

Mildew

Mildew may develop on wet furniture. To remove:

Brush with a broom to remove loose mold from outer covering. Do this outdoors so you won't scatter mildew spores, which can start new growth.

Vacuum the surface to draw out mold. Dispose of the vacuum cleaner bag outside to avoid scattering mold spores indoors.

If mildew remains and fabric is washable, sponge lightly with thick soap or detergent suds. Wipe with a clean, damp cloth. Get as little water on the fabric as possible, so the padding doesn't get wet.

If mold remains, wipe the furniture with a damp cloth dipped in diluted alcohol (1 cup denatured alcohol to 1 cup water) or chlorine bleach solution (teaspoon bleach to a cup of water). Test in an area that isn't obvious.

Dry the article thoroughly.

Use a spray containing a fungicide to get rid of musty odors and any remaining mildew. Moisten all surfaces thoroughly. Spray frequently if mildew is a continuing problem.

If mold has grown into inner parts,

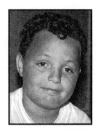

Randy Martinez,
Age 9

"Make sure all the doors are locked real tight so the hurricane won't get in your house."

F.F. Judson

"The roof is the most important feature that saves a house from considerable damage. To reinforce the roof, a metal U-shaped retention strip should be invented. These strips should be nailed and sealed on top of and parallel to the drip strips on all new roof slope edges.

When the roof is shingled, the shingle ends should be pushed into this strip and nailed as usual. Covering the ends of the shingles on the roof pitch would greatly assist in holding the weakest part of the roof at a minimal cost."

send furniture to a dry cleaner or storage company for thorough drying and fumigation. Fumigation will kill mold present at the time, but will not protect against future attacks.

Wood Furniture

Wood furniture can best be salvaged through slow drying and proper repair.

Take furniture outdoors and remove as many drawers, slides and removable parts as possible. Drawers and doors may be stuck shut. Do not try to force them out. After allowing to dry for a brief period, use a screwdriver or chisel to remove the backs and push out the drawers from behind.

After you have removed the parts, clean off mud and dirt, using a hose if necessary.

Take furniture indoors and store it where it will dry slowly. Furniture left in sunlight to dry will warp.

Glue And Clamps

When furniture is dry, re-glue it if necessary. You will need woodworking tools and clamps to re-glue some pieces. Before you start, decide whether you have the time, equipment and ability to do the work. Consult an experienced cabinetmaker if necessary.

To re-glue loose joints, thoroughly clean them of old glue, following directions on container. Hold parts together with rope tourniquets or suitable clamps. To prevent damage from ropes or clamps, pad them with cloth.

White spots or a cloudy film may develop on furniture that has gotten damp. To remove the spots:

If the entire surface is affected, rub with a damp cloth dipped in turpentine or camphorated oil, or in a solution of one

half cup household ammonia and one half cup water. Wipe dry at once and polish with wax or furniture polish.

If color is not restored, dip 3/0 steel wool in oil (boiled linseed, olive, mineral or lemon). Rub lightly with the wood grain. Wipe with a soft cloth and re-wax.

Removing Spots

For deep spots, use a drop or two of ammonia on a damp cloth. Rub at once with a dry cloth. Polish. Rubbing cigarette ashes, powdered pumice or a piece of walnut into spots may help remove them.

If spots still remain, the piece should be stripped and refinished.

Veneered Furniture

Thoroughly dry furniture. If veneer is loose in a few places, carefully scrape glue under loose areas.

Press veneer back in place. Place wax paper over affected area and heat with warm iron. Remove iron and place weights on area.

If veneering doesn't stay in place or is bubbled, carefully slit the loose veneer with a razor blade and apply a good glue. Ask for advice at the hardware store. Cover the glued spots with wax paper and then place something heavy over the area while the glue dries.

If your insurance allows partial reimbursement for flood-damaged furniture, it may be worthwhile to apply the money to new furniture, rather than pay for extensive repairs.

Pitch or Save? Upholstered furniture may be salvageable if you can clean it and get all the mildew out. But extensively damaged pieces may need new padding or may have to be replaced altogether.

Claudia Perez,
Age 9

"When I found out we were going to have a hurricane, I felt frightened. I had never been through a hurricane before. My family and I huddled in the hall. We heard the wind swishing by. We also heard things banging around. I had never been more frightened in my life. I stayed up all night and just sat up thinking. I didn't think I would make it, but I did. I finally fell asleep. I woke up in the morning and walked outside. Everything was thrown around. Later, I got dressed and helped my parents, brother and sister pick up all the branches. We then rode around to see the damage. I cried while we rode by."

Leon Rolle

"Miami has been very fortunate in the past. Unfortunately, they need to revamp the South Florida Building Code. A lot of places in South Dade should never have been built. Homes have been built on filled-in mangrove swamps. Overdevelopment contributed to the loss."

Adjusters

Finally, after all the days of waiting, the insurance adjuster arrives at your house. How do you deal with this person? What should you expect? What are your rights?

Here are some typical questions and answers compiled with help from insurance consultants:

Q. I have a TV set that I bought for $700 in 1980. It's ruined. How much will the insurance company pay?

A. It depends on the kind of policy you bought. If you have an "actual cash value" policy, the company might allow you $700, but then depreciate the amount for the time the set has been in use. You might not get much. But if you have a "full replacement cost" policy, with its higher yearly premiums, the company must buy you a new TV set of equal brand and quality, even if inflation has pushed up its price to $1,200 today. But the rule is this: If the company gives you the $1,200, you must actually buy the new set. You can't just take the money and go on a vacation to Bermuda.

Q. Say a natural wood ceiling is water-stained. It's still structurally solid, and the damage is purely cosmetic. Can you insist the insurance company replace the wood at a very high price, or will it make you live with the ugliness?

A. It's a negotiation, like buying a car. Insurance companies are obliged to repair or replace such damaged items to restore them to their condition before the storm. But this is where the "prudent-man rule" comes into play. Would a prudent person replace the wood, or would he or she sand it, stain it a bit darker and live with it? If it's too close to

call, you might negotiate — say, give up on a new ceiling but ask the adjuster to give you a bit more money for some damaged plaster ceilings.

Q. Does the adjuster look over your house, hand you a check and leave forever?

A. Not likely. The process is too complicated. Probably the adjuster will give you an interim check on the spot so you can do things like giving your roofing contractor a down payment to buy materials. Then after all the repairs are finished, you can submit the actual bills and get a final check for the difference.

Q. Is there any way I can speed the process?

A. Sure. Be ready when the adjuster arrives. Have ready a precise, neatly written list of damage. Include the name of the damaged item, its price when new and the year you bought it. If you can find a receipt, give the adjuster that, too. The more detail you provide, the quicker and more accurate the appraisal will be. If you can't find a receipt, call around to stores and ask for ballpark prices.

Q. What percentage of my roof must be damaged before the insurance company will pay for a new roof?

A. It's based on overall damage. If one-third of the shingles are gone, and they can be replaced and the roof made watertight without replacing the other two-thirds, that's what the insurer will do. The company has to find shingles that match the color — or at least that match it after about a year of aging and blending.

Q. If I have a set of Royal Daulton china in a discontinued pattern, and I lose just two plates, will my insurer buy me a whole new set?

A. Yes, if your insurance policy has the relatively standard "pairs and sets" clause. It means that if you lose just one earring, the company has to buy you a set if you can't find a match for the lost earring. But if the company does buy you a set of earrings, it will probably want to keep your single earring so you don't make an undeserved profit on the transaction.

Q. If you have to move out of the house while roofers or plasterers work, will the insurance company pay for your hotel?

A. Again, the "prudent-man" rule applies. If the house is unsafe or unhealthy, the company will pay for your hotel room. If it's merely an inconvenience, it won't. Here's where you negotiate again.

Q. If I don't think my insurance adjuster is giving me enough money, can I appeal?

A. Sure, in several ways, in this order: First, you can ask your insurance agent to put you in touch with a senior adjuster or supervisory adjuster.

If that doesn't work, many insurance policies allow arbitration. You hire an arbitrator. The insurance company hires an arbitrator. The two get together and try to work out a reasonable solution.

The next step is to hire a public adjuster. He represents you in dealing with the insurance adjuster for a percentage of any additional money he gets you. But think before hiring one. Your previously cooperative, friendly insurance company is going to become instantly less accommodating if it sees a public adjuster coming.

Q. It's three weeks after the storm. How long is it reasonable to wait for an adjuster?

A. Up to a month might be reasonable in an overwhelming situation.

Don't Move: After a storm, washing is harder to do, but more important than usual.

Ezequiel Olvera,
Age 11

"It will be like a bad dream so you need to put your stuff in a box and keep it near you so it doesn't fly away. If you lose your toys you won't have anything to play with after the hurricane."

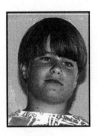

Michael Reynolds,
Age 10

"Don't panic. Go to a closet or the bathroom and just wait there. It will be scary but you'll be OK."

Contractors

Cool down when dealing with contractors, experts say. Conduct yourself in a formal, businesslike manner. Contractors are not your friends — they are doing a job for you. Document every transaction. Demand accountability.

If you have a contract and paid upfront, only to have your contractor slack off or vanish, consider your options:

■ Take steps to make the contractor more accountable so the remaining work is completed properly.

■ Fire the contractor. This entails ending the contract. Talk to a lawyer to ensure you cover all of the legal ramifications and at least break even.

Take Charge

These suggestions will help you regain control over your home reconstruction or put your case together if you need to go to court.

Send a demand letter to your contractor via certified mail. Specify the problems you want addressed. For example: ''You told me three weeks ago you were getting building permits for the living room. I haven't heard from you since. I would like copies of the permits or an explanation why you don't have them.''

Set a deadline for the contractor to respond, and say when and where you can be reached. Example: ''Please respond within seven days. I can be reached at (phone number) between noon and 1 p.m. Monday through Friday.'' Choose times when you can have a witness — a co-worker, a friend or a relative — with you. When the contractor calls you, say you will have a witness to the conversation.

Ask for a written response from the contractor to follow up the conversation.

Provide the contractor with a certified letter that documents what was promised and agreed to in the conversation.

Keep Records

Keep copies of all correspondence. If your contractor refuses certified mail, keep copies of the refusals. Gather copies of all contracts, canceled checks, building permits and any other documents relating to the construction work.

Withhold payment for any incomplete work. Refuse requests for large amounts of advance money to pay for materials. Good contractors have working capital and credit to get supplies. You may agree to pay for portions of the work as each portion gets completed.

Withhold 10 percent of payment for work done until the contractor provides you with an inspection certificate, warranty of work, a release of lien and affidavits saying all subcontractors used have been paid for that portion of the work.

File Complaint

Report contractors who don't keep their side of the contract to the Department of Professional Regulation. Although it takes time for the agency to complete investigations, it will follow through and penalize contractors who break the rules. Call 377-7115 between 8 a.m. and 4 p.m. and ask for the construction duty officer. Tell the officer you want to file a complaint. They will mail you a complaint form, which you must fill out, sign and return.

Consider hiring your own attorney. If the relationship with your contractor is beyond repair, your only recourse to recover for work that never was done may be a lawsuit.

Caring For Trees

If you're able to tackle landscaping cleanup after the storm, here's what you can do to help your trees recover:

Don't wash off any remaining soil on the roots.

Wrap the roots with moist towels, burlap, sheets or blankets; or cover with soil from another area of the yard. The key is to prevent sun and air exposure, which will burn and dry the roots. Never wrap the roots in plastic: It will cook them.

Keep the roots moist until replanting.

If you want to re-stand the tree yourself, landscapers advise a 15- to 20-foot tree with a 6-inch diameter is about the maximum size you can handle without machinery or a truck.

In preparing the tree for replanting, you may want to prune it to ease handling. But do not chop off the top. Use caution, trees can snap back dangerously.

There are three key aspects to replanting: removal of air pockets from the root ball, the root depth and supporting the tree:

Air pockets: These may be trapped between the roots and any dirt clinging to them. Poke a garden hose through the root system before replanting, and water lightly until it flows evenly.

Root depth: The root system should be returned to its original depth in the ground. To accomplish this, try digging out the tree's hole on the opposite side from which it fell.

Support the tree: You can use 2-by-4s, 1-by-6s, wire or rope. Don't nail anything into the tree trunk. Wrap towels around the trunk before you brace any boards against it.

Put soil over the replanted roots.

Expect to keep the tree staked for six months.

Water as if you are planting a new tree. Thoroughly water every day for a week, and then every other day for several weeks. Mulch to a depth of three inches to help retain soil moisture.

Protect the newly exposed trunk and branches from sunburn. Dilute water-based latex paint and coat the limbs and parts of the trunk that have been shaded for many years. Sunburn may cause the bark to blister. It may affect the tree immediately or it could take a year or longer.

Do not use wound paint on the pruning wounds or on the bark. In this humid, hot climate, wound paint could trap bacteria and fungus inside the tree and cause more damage than it was intended to prevent.

Don't fertilize until the trees have had a chance to start new root growth and become established again, sending out one or two new flushes of leaves.

How They Fared

Landscapers and tree trimmers said these trees suffered the most during Hurricane Andrew:

Black olive
Acacia
Ficus (if it was hat-racked)
Sea grape
Tabebuia

The reasons include too-shallow root systems, particularly for trees atop coral rock, and hat-racking, in which trees were pruned so heavily that they had many bare limbs sticking up. New growth then creates a dense canopy that is overly resistant to wind.

Trees that stood up better include:
Sabal palms
Thrinax palms
Live oaks

Roy Tyson

"One of the things that helped was planting trees, especially planting fruit trees to help protect the building. The storm will hit trees first and protect your home. If I could say anything else, I would tell people to get three estimates on the work that needs to be done — that's a good policy."

Maren Sachs,
Age 10

"Fill your tub with water because your toilets won't work and your water will be contaminated. Usually, you will need to go food shopping. Please, let me warn you. The stores will be jam packed and food will be scarce so buy your food in advance. In my case it helped. My family stocked up with instant milk. Yuck! I think you should stock up with things that won't spoil. Remember to stay in a closed area with no windows. Follow these precautions and you will be very safe."

Dade County slash pines
Canary Island date palms
Washingtonia palms
Gumbo-limbo
Old, established royal poincianas

Cutting Back: Heavy pruning may be needed to get a top-heavy tree back up when half its root system has been destroyed. Handle the broken limbs first by cutting back to the nearest sound wood V-crotch.

Down, But Not Out

Trees uprooted by a hurricane can be successfully righted even after several weeks of being on their sides provided roots have been kept shaded and dampened. This allows time to evaluate the damage and wait for help from a reputable tree service or arborist rather than hastily destroying them.

When sizing up tree damage, you may find the central leader snapped off and limbs ripped away with pieces of the main trunk. Should you save these? Ask yourself three questions: How much do you value the tree? If you save it, will it ever have a form that will withstand wind and be a viable tree? What else in the landscape requires attention and is this particular tree worth it?

What's Worth Saving

If the tree has lost 50 or 60 percent or more of its canopy, you may want to consider eliminating it. Smaller and less damaged trees may prove healthier in the long run. But if you want to save a rare tree temporarily, while growing a replacement, prune it as little as possible — just enough to make it safe — and allow new shoots to sprout.

New shoots will help produce new roots, and you may succeed in getting your damaged specimen to flower and set seed, from which you can begin again. Or, you can purchase another smaller tree and eliminate the crippled one in a few years when the small one grows up.

When half of a tree's root system has been destroyed, heavy pruning may be necessary just to get the top-heavy tree back up and propped in place. Deal with broken limbs first by cutting back to the nearest sound wood V-crotch, where the branch forks. If 50 percent of that joint still has bark intact, you can consider it a sound wood crotch.

Cut Carefully

If you have to take a major limb back to the trunk, cut just beyond the branch collar. Clean off ragged branches to a smooth cut so water runs off, but don't worry about this part of the job immediately if there's a lot of work to be done just righting other trees. The secondary pruning can be done in the months ahead.

If whole sections of a tree were blown out, balance the canopy so the tree is safe and able to withstand future wind, but allow the tree to grow back for a year or more before trying to create a symmetrical canopy. Where one limb has been broken in a canopy, others are likely to break, so examine the tree carefully for vertical splits in the bark and limbs that may not show damage at first glance. While a tree could survive with such cracks, it's better to remove the limb or even the whole tree if the cracks are pervasive.

Save Leaves

Where bark has been ripped away, take a chisel or knife and smooth the edge. Cut away loose bark only as needed, enlarging the wound as little as possible to hasten the covering-over process.

Save as many leaves as possible. These are the photosynthesis factories that drive the life of the tree. There will be a flush of leaves right after a hurricane, and these may die back. The first flush is sometimes fueled by reserve carbohydrates in the bark and roots. Once those reserves are depleted, the leaves may die. Yet, the temporary leaves will begin the rebuilding process, and the second set of leaves (if

Katie Musich,
Age 10

"Throughout Hurricane Andrew, I felt very mad and sad at the same time. It almost felt like I had to cry. The first time I went outside it was weird. I am always used to swinging on a swing or playing or climbing a tree, but it wasn't like that at all. It was all dead and unhappy. I couldn't stop thinking about the past and when I hear rainstorms I relive Andrew, but in fear. I try to hide my feelings but just can't sometimes. I often wonder why it had to happen to me, and not somebody else. But I'll never forget the morning when people were helping people. We all will live to tell that on Aug. 24, 1992, our lives changed forever."

**Emily Marckioli,
Age 9**

"Before Hurricane Andrew I looked outside my house and I thought, 'I hope it looks this way afterwards.' I was scared when my dad woke me up at 1 a.m. to say 'Get dressed. It is getting worse.' My sister and I walked outside before Andrew and when we came in the power was shut off. During the hurricane I was sitting on the couch with my grandma and my sister. My dad and my brother were holding the door shut. We had to shift into my room because the window in the living room would not shut. I was scared when the huge ficus tree fell on our house and my puppy was sitting near the window. After Andrew was over it was horrible. We had nothing. I hated it."

this occurs) will continue it.

Don't panic over downed or damaged trees and eliminate them completely. Many can recover with the right care that includes lots of water for several weeks after the storm to encourage new root development and light fertilizer in the spring.

Prudent Painting, Pruning

Don't use black, gooey pruning paint. This can seal in fungus and disease or later crack open to allow disease entry.

Don't hat rack. An enormous number of trees were senselessly reduced to stumps right after Hurricane Andrew. Hat-racking produces a lot of weakly attached limbs that tend to be thicker than before such pruning. It will be necessary to thin these masses of shoots the following year to prevent windtoss, and even the remaining limbs won't be as strong as the originals.

If severe pruning is necessary, and the trunks or limbs have not been exposed to sunlight in a long time, paint the newly exposed bark with a diluted water-based white latex to avoid sunburn. Sunburn may destroy the cambial tissue just beneath the bark that produces new growth. It also can fry the water-carrying tissues below that, resulting in gradual death of whole sections of the tree.

On the Way Back: Don't give up on downed or damaged trees. Lots of water after the storm and light fertilizer in the spring will help them make a comeback.

Palm Care

Palms stood up better throughout Hurricane Andrew than hardwood trees, thanks to their flexible trunks. Nonetheless, you can help palms recover from the brutal internal beating they take in a hurricane.

As with hardwoods, examine overturned palms and determine what can be reset with success rather than waste time and money on plants that have little or no chance of surviving.

When only a petticoat of roots remains on the fringe of the trunk, this may be a sign that ganoderms or butt rot has already invaded your palm. This disease affects many palms in South Florida, weakening them. Coconuts, phoenix palms, ptychospermas, royals, Washingtonias — a total of 23 palm genera are susceptible to that fungus, which moves underground.

If your toppled palms have this petticoat of roots and you want to nurse them back, go ahead. But it may be a long recovery.

Be sure to treat the roots of these and other re-planted palms with a fungicide.

No Nails In Trunk

When propping palms, use burlap-coated short pieces of 2- by-4s strapped to the trunk and nail longer props into these. Never drive nails directly into a palm trunk. The wounds will not heal and are an invitation to disease. If frond stems are broken at the base, cut them off.

Remember, though, that palms can transfer needed minerals from old leaves into new and developing ones. So leave as many healthy leaves on your palms as possible.

The exception is heavy-headed palms, such as coconuts, which may have all the fronds blown to one side, making it difficult to keep the specimen upright. Cut off enough fronds to stabilize the palm in the ground.

Test Crown

Another tip: Pull some of the fronds on a fallen coconut or other heavy-headed palm, and see if the crown moves in the top of the trunk before you go to the trouble of resetting it. If the crown has been knocked loose, don't re-plant.

Removing fronds opens up entryways for disease, so keep that in mind as well. Additionally, Latania palms are susceptible to palm weevils. Do as little trimming as possible on these palms, or you'll invite an almost immediate invasion. Palm weevils — which also attack sabal and phoenix palms — are big, dark weevils, about one inch long, with noticeably extended snouts. Some have burgundy on their backs. Fairchild Tropical Garden used Cygon on palms to ward off the weevils, but this is an extremely potent pesticide so use it cautiously.

Don't Drench Roots

Reset palms, leaving as many roots as possible, put soil around the bases, and water. But don't overwater because without many healthy roots, the base can be prone to root rot. Moist but not soggy is good advice for palm roots as well as house plants.

Water every other day for a few weeks. Don't let the root ball become totally dry during the next few months that it will take for palms to become re-established.

Treat the crowns with a fungicide. Bud rot is common after a hurricane, the palm experts said, because pathogens are blown

David Verdi,
Age 18

"I'd want to stay, but I wouldn't go to a shelter, I wouldn't feel comfortable there. I'd make sure all my valuable things were put away, so they didn't get ruined."

Ian Maguire,
Age 17

"I think I would stay. My house did pretty well, so I think I'd be safe there. It was a really bad experience, but in a way it did some good. It changed a lot of people's attitudes for the better. I guess being totally helpless will do that."

from the soil to the air and can land in the crown.

Use copper fungicide and Manzate, one tablespoon each in a gallon of water, as a spray or drench poured into the crown if you can reach it. Copper has an antibacterial effect; Manzate, or the mancozeb fungicides, also contain zinc, a micronutrient needed by plants, particularly palms, and has antibacterial activity as well.

Recovery Period

You can mix some 20-20-20 or other water-soluble fertilizer in the fungicide spray for palm crowns, but don't apply granular fertilizer to the roots now. Wait to give roots a chance to develop and recover. If a hurricane is followed by heavy rains, you may want to apply a light fertilizer (about a quarter the normal application) in October to the side of the palm that was not taken out of the ground or lightly around palms that were not toppled. Or, you can safely wait until March.

New spears may be deformed or sunburned after a hurricane. And it may take a year for palms to completely recover — or to show damage that's undetectable immediately after the storm.

Smile: Even in the worst of times, Dade County residents never lost hope or their sense of humor.